THE EDUCATION

of

DISADVANTAGED CHILDREN

THE EDUCATION

of

DISADVANTAGED CHILDREN

Raymond Bottom

Parker Publishing Company, Inc.

West Nyack, New York

Library of Congress
Catalog Card Number: 74-96296

PRINTED IN THE UNITED STATES OF AMERICA
B & P – 13-236513-8

A Word from the Author
About the Practical Nature of This Book

The principal who earns his pay is a busy man. He doesn't have time to read the stacks of professional materials that inundate his desk. This book deals with specific problems that face the principal—apathy, academic deficits, hostility, poor self-image, lack of motivation, truancy, stealing, and other garden variety of "challenges"—and provides guidelines, suggestions and practical tips for solving these problems.

While we will deal primarily with administering the disadvantaged school, nearly every principal faces the problem of how to set up a realistic, relevant educational program for children of the poor. In the many schools where the underprivileged are in the minority, they constitute a different kind of problem since discrepancies between them and their middle-class peers are so marked. The practical solutions found here will provide the principal with answers to his frustrated teachers' question: "What in the world can I do for them?"

The first section of the book deals with the initial selection of teachers who have the particular skills necessary for most effective instruction of the disadvantaged. Emphasis will be placed on the development of teamwork, and applying practical solutions to some of the more disturbing problems that occur with parents, pupils and staff members.

The special needs of the disadvantaged will be covered, including ways to evaluate their progress and the development of innovative programs designed to capture their interest and imagination. Practical approaches to disciplinary techniques are included, as well as methods to consider for development of the community school program, extending the program throughout the summer months. Finally, guidelines are offered that will help insure the most effective use of federal aid for program improvement—including ways to measure specific results in planning for the future.

Education is constantly on the move and, as always, the principal is in the forefront of the action. He is the key to needed changes. He respects the value of the old but constantly searches for new and better ways to meet the increasing needs of every student. This book is written to offer productive ideas, based on actual experience, that will help the principal in his role as an educational leader—particularly with respect to those often desperate students who are referred to as the "disadvantaged."

R.B.

Table of Contents

Providing Special Help

The Role of Special Services Personnel

Approaches and Teaching Ideas That Work

Making Reading Come Alive · Interest Arousing Approaches · Individual Pupil Work Plans · Using Trips to Teach

Summary

Arriving at a Testing Philosophy

Finding Teacher Opinions · Parents Should Be Asked · Don't Forget to Ask the Children

Providing an Effective Group Testing Committee

Selection of Members · Functions of the Testing Committee · Interpreting the Program

Important Factors in Assessment of Disadvantaged Students

Teacher Made Tests · Reporting Standardized Test Results to Parents · Holding Grade Conferences with Pupils · Using Student Self-Evaluation · Developing a Promotion Policy · Utilizing the Verbal Report

Summary

Identifying Problem Areas · Establishing a Planning Committee · Techniques That Aid Innovation · The Importance of Follow-Up

The Cross-Age Pupil Tutoring Program

The First Year · Subsequent Years · Cautions to Be Observed

Summary

Providing Facilities · Renovating Existing Structures · Selecting Library Personnel · Selecting Library Aides · Selecting Materials · Some Final Considerations in Materials Selection · Providing for Maximum Library Use · Encouraging Parent Use · Evaluating the Library Program

Summary

1

Selection and Retention of Teachers for the Disadvantaged

The effective school principal is a generalist. The position requires myriad duties and responsibilities and the principal must develop the knack of handling large and small problems with equal facility. In the course of one day he may spend time talking to a parent group about educational plans that involve thousands of dollars and search for a safety pin to temporarily repair split trousers. With the immense range of responsibilities, certain areas must be given priority. Among other jobs he does, human relations stands out as one of the most important. Like it or not, we are all judged by how effectively we deal with the human side of students, teachers and parents.

Nowhere is this skill more important, especially in disadvantaged schools, than in the recruitment of new teachers. Educators are all agreed that the most important cog in the educational machine is the classroom teacher.

Professional ball teams long ago discovered that the secret of success lies in recruiting. Every team has thus developed an elaborate system for discovering and developing new talent. Certainly we in education should pay as much attention to recruiting as a ball club. When we consider that every elementary teacher may be exposed to a thousand or more children in his teaching career, we simply can't afford less than the best recruiting program to attract and develop teaching talent.

Finding Teacher Talent

The first axiom of teacher recruiting is to go where the teachers are. In a competitive market no school system can sit back and wait for teacher candidates to come to them and expect to get top-notch personnel. In many systems a Director of Personnel or an Assistant Superintendent is in charge of recruiting. However, the wide awake principal will ask to be included in personnel recruitment for his building. The extra work involved in recruiting sorties can pay off for years when excellent teachers are the result. Every principal who has been burdened with a teacher who "didn't fit in" knows how many hours of frustration can be spent trying to salvage a poor initial selection. Like marriage, the quest for new staff members should be a thoughtful process that involves the opportunity to be exposed to more than one choice.

Working as a team with the chief recruiter allows the system to cover more recruiting territory. This has merit, for many systems recruit too much from only a few colleges and face the problem of insularity. Good staff composition results when many colleges and geographical areas are represented. New people and new ideas are often the catalysts the principal needs to give a final nudge to a movement toward needed change. Teachers from different geographical areas are especially valuable to the education of underprivileged children. Many have never been beyond the boundaries of their city or county and have little conception of the customs and mores of other parts of our country.

The principal who is a "step ahead" identifies his needs early. He establishes soon after the first semester which teachers do not intend to return the following year. With this information he can analyze class composition, student weaknesses and strengths and come up with a fair idea of the type of personality he would like as a replacement. While this is no guarantee he will get exactly what he is looking for, it is much better than the "hit and miss" system employed by too many school systems.

THE CANDIDATE INTERVIEW

The teacher shortage has created a seller's market. The interview often becomes a one way street with the recruiter trying to influence the candidate without asking searching questions of his own. In such an interview topics such as the cultural and recreational offerings of the community and available apartments may get more coverage than the educational program.

The principal of the disadvantaged school cannot settle for a pleasant chat. He must ferret out basic attitudes and look for experience factors that will spell success or defeat in working with underprivileged children.

Important Basic Attitudes and Qualities

The teacher who fails with disadvantaged children does so because of lack of certain vital personal qualities. The successful teacher, above all, genuinely likes and accepts his students. Some teachers mistake tolerance for liking but they don't fool the kids. These children are experts at spotting phonies and they have various methods of getting back at the "pretenders."

Warmth and a sense of humor must be present to help both students and teacher over the rough spots that lie ahead.

Understanding and empathy are essential qualities. The breakfast he didn't have, the sleep he didn't get, the family fight he shouldn't have seen or the cuff he didn't deserve can make Johnny an unresponsive or belligerent student on any given day. It takes a mature person to stand up to a sudden outburst of "I hate you" from an emotionally upset child. Confidence in his own ability and a sense of personal security can help a teacher handle such a situation.

The middle-class molds simply won't fit a room of children who have had to learn to live by the code of the street. The inflexible teacher who can't improvise, cope with the unexpected, and roll with the punches is sure misery for his students and himself.

Discipline is a fact of life in the disadvantaged school. Every day brings problems, unpleasantness and confrontation. Stability, firmness and quiet strength are qualities that work best with youngsters who have been exposed all their lives to inconsistency, harshness and loudness.

Every principal has learned the sad fact that some candidates project well in an interview and then fail to measure up in the classroom. The principal who is uncertain about a prospective teacher can ask him to complete a series of open ended questions. Examples of such questions might be:

1. Underprivileged children are . . .
2. Culturally disadvantaged students' attitudes toward school and teachers are . . .
3. In dealing with parents of disadvantaged children the teacher should . . .
4. To establish order in a disadvantaged school a teacher must . . .

Answers to these and other similar questions can be a valuable supplement to an oral interview.

Helpful Experience and Background

Nobody is at more of a disadvantage than the beginning teacher in a disadvantaged school. The first day he is burdened with all the fears and unknowns of every beginning teacher. Unlike his counterpart in the middle-class school, however, he does not have a few days' grace to feel his way. The students who face him the first day give no quarter. They take advantage of every mistake he makes. Obviously the more he knows about his students the fewer first week errors he will commit.

Pre-preparation of teachers for the disadvantaged schools is generally lacking. However, some colleges and universities do have affiliations with disadvantaged schools for student teachers, and others encourage and aid future teachers to work in some capacity with the deprived.

The best prepared candidates are those who have done practice teaching in disadvantaged schools. They have acquired basic understanding of the students they will teach. The fact that they desire to continue teaching the deprived is usually indicative of the right attitudes and needed strengths.

Candidates whose only experience was gained from Head Start, tutoring deprived students, or working in neighborhood projects lack vital classroom experience. However, they have had the opportunity to gain valuable insights into the children's outlook and behavior characteristics that will help them in their teaching.

Certainly not to be overlooked is the candidate who was reared in a deprived neighborhood. He knows every facet of the community and can be a valuable resource person for the principal in his relations with the community at large. If the candidate is returning to his home school, he can often open doors that are closed to all other school personnel. He also represents living proof to his students that those with ambition and desire can rise above the level of the slum neighborhood.

No mention has been made of the prospective teacher's academic credentials. These should be examined, of course, for good grades are indicative of intelligence, good work habits and persistence. However, academic qualifications are not nearly as important as proper attitudes toward and knowledge of the deprived child.

Tell the Whole Truth

If the principal is sold on the candidate and the candidate is sold on the school, the applicant should be told *all* the facts. If the building is old and lacks facilities, he should be informed. If materials are in short supply, it should not be held from him. Above all, if he has no experience in working with the disadvantaged, a clear explanation of the situation should be given him.

The new teacher who walks into the classroom uninformed and unprepared undergoes a case of "cultural shock" from which he may never recover. Illustrative of this is the teacher from a strict middle-class background who hadn't the slightest idea of what the disadvantaged child was like or how to teach him. Her middle-class sensibilities were shocked and the first week was spent making mountains out of molehills. Students were punished for slouching in seats, laughing at the wrong times, and putting their legs in the aisle. A major blowup occurred when she heard a fairly mild epithet. Unable to bend, understand or like the kids, she became the target for all they could dish out. This teacher left as soon as a substitute could be found to replace her.

Clearing Up Misconceptions

A great number of graduating teachers have gained their knowledge of the poor through reading. There is a danger they may have categorized *all* deprived students as prone to lie, steal, cheat and fight. They may think every student is indifferent to school, hostile to authority, and unable to do grade level work.

This is simply not so, and the wise principal will quickly set the prospective teacher straight. On the elementary level the majority of students like school and indicate that they enjoy themselves while attending. Some, though not as many as in middle-class schools, are excellent students. Most parents have an interest in their children's progress although this interest is not nearly as likely to result in parental help as it does in middle-class homes. The kids have a tougher front but basically they're not too much different from other children, and they *can* be reached by the right teacher.

The principal's task is to select the right raw product and help mold him into a finished, effective teacher through a thorough orientation and a continuous in-service program.

ORIENTATING NEW TEACHERS

First Help Them Get Settled

Once the new teacher has inked the contract the red carpet should not be rolled up and hidden away. If the principal is available during the summer, he should offer help in getting his new teachers settled.

The importance of acquainting the newcomers with the community should not be overlooked. Helping arrange for church and club affiliations, recommending doctors and dentists, and other necessary potpourri of living can make the settling down process much quicker and more enjoyable. A pre-school "Getting to Know You" picnic of all building teachers is an excellent way of introducing new staff members to their colleagues.

Throughout the year, periodic evening get-togethers for new staff members can serve the dual purpose of offering the opportunity to socialize and share common problems. The principal and selected experienced staff members are present to listen, answer questions and offer suggestions.

Giving the Facts

No beginning teacher is prepared for the avalanche of regulations, policies and forms that bury him the first week of school. His first natural impulse is to give up or he is so overwhelmed he spends time on paper work that should be spent preparing for students that all-important first week.

A sad but true fact exists that many administrators can offer only a one day pre-school orientation session for new teachers. When faced with this problem, the principal should place emphasis on the human aspect—learning about the pupils' background and needs, how to control and motivate them, and ways to organize for effective instruction. However, to put matters in their proper perspective, a two or three day orientation for new teachers should be considered minimal. When adequate time is allowed, the following program can be used to induce first year teachers to make those crucial first steps in the right direction.

Explanations of necessary school forms should be dispensed with first. Carefully explain which forms are necessary at the beginning and which can wait. Start at this point emphasizing that students come first.

The time spent on the school's written policies may save hours and misunderstanding at a later time. Policies are a legitimate form of orientation since they inform new staff members, clarify their relationships, and delineate duties and responsibilities.

Even though the beginning teacher may exhibit little interest in the tenure process, its purposes, responsibilities and how it can be achieved should be explained. The teacher sponsor-probationer relationship can be a rewarding one if the proper match is made. The new teacher should understand that the primary duty of his sponsor is to help him adjust to the school. The beginner should be encouraged to utilize his sponsor to the fullest as an advisor. Not all sponsor-probationer relationships are as successful as Sears-Roebuck, and the beginner should understand that new assignments can be made if a match proves unfruitful.

Facing Teacher Concerns

The awesome experience of walking into a classroom and facing 25 or more unknown quantities lies just ahead, and understandably the neophyte is a little shaky.

The new teacher has a long list of concerns and these should be faced before school opens. At least part of one day should be set aside for questions. If possible, one or more experienced staff members should be on hand to help provide answers.

From past experience the principal can anticipate most questions. A prepared booklet with the most common questions and answers is a source of relief to the new member. He knows that others have faced the same concerns and have managed to cope with them. A sure bet to pop up in every question and answer session is this number one concern:

Q. How do I gain and maintain classroom control?

A. Be firm from the first minute. Make few rules but enforce the ones you have. Don't see everything. Learn to overlook the little things. Ask for help from the principal, counselor and school social worker on major or persistent problems. A booklet on classroom discipline is included in your opening day folder. This topic will be covered fully at the all staff orientation by the principal and other school personnel.

Other questions that arise year after year are:

Where do I find supplementary materials?
How do I go about getting teaching supplies?
Where can I get audiovisiual aids?
Are field trips allowed?
Who runs the duplicator and mimeo, the teacher or secretary?
Do I have a money allotment to spend for my room?
How do I handle sick children?
What do I do about chronic tardiness and absences?
Is there help for children with inadequate food and clothes?
How do I arrange for conferences with parents?

The beginner is only a beginner and there are other problem areas unknown to him of which he should be aware. Now is the time to stress the importance of the cumulative folder and the invaluable information it contains. Up to this point the new teacher has thought of the disadvantaged child as one large composite group. In his mind he pictures a tough kid with problems achieving below grade level. From this time on he must see each child as an individual with unique problems and potentialities. Using the cumulative folder he can acquire a fairly accurate picture of each student before he walks into the classroom. Later, knowledge of the child and contacts with the home will help complete the picture.

Listening to the Voice of Experience

Important in dealing with classroom problems is an understanding of basic causes, and possible appropriate action. Experience, as no other factor, gives the answer for handling the deprived child. A panel of experienced teachers using the following format is effective in providing some answers.

Problem: Johnny refuses to read when requested.

Basic Cause: Johnny may be unable to read at grade level. In every elementary grade there are some children that are practically nonreaders.

Possible Action: Check his cumulative folder first. If he is an extremely poor reader, give him a way out of his present predicament and try to find appropriate materials for future work. Inquire about the possibilities of special help from the remedial reading teacher.

Problem: Susie won't do her assigned work. Instead she annoys others who are trying to work.

Basic Cause: Susie may have emotional problems or she may be testing you.

Possible Action: Check her cumulative folder. Any information from previous teachers on emotional problems? If so, don't push until you have the opportunity to seek help from the school social service worker. If there is no previous history of emotional problems, accept the challenge. Inform Susie she will work during recess, that you intend to talk to the principal and her parents about her lack of cooperativeness. Quick, firm action can stop others who may have ideas similar to Susie's.

Problem: Jane comes to school dirty. She has a terrible body odor.

Basic Cause: Jane's problem is economic. Her house lacks indoor plumbing and her mother has four children under school age to take care of.

Possible Action: Take an interest in Jane. Stress the benefits of cleanliness in health classes and how it can be attained *without* a bathroom. Report Jane's inadequate clothes to the principal. He has a source of supply.

Problem: Jim talks in a loud threatening manner every time he is displeased. When reprimanded he tries to talk over the teacher.

Basic Cause: Jim lives in a loud world. He has learned to talk over crying babies, blaring radios and televisions, and other household noises. Jim has often been denied the right to present his side of the story to adults.

Possible Action: Assure the class, and Jim in particular, that they will be allowed to defend their actions but insist that it be done in reasonable tones. If subsequent shouting occurs, attach some penalty for failure to observe a reasonable rule.

Problem: Jerry misses school excessively. He never brings an excuse.

Basic Cause: Jerry may be taking the easy way out of a frustrating situation or he may be required to stay home for family responsibilities.

Possible Action: Make certain Jerry is not being asked to work above his ability level. Try to get close to him. Find his interests and work with him there. In the meantime, make certain the principal is made aware of the problem. If the family is keeping him home the principal or truant office will take care of the problem.

Problem: Tom has been involved in one fight after another.

Basic Cause: Excessive fighting may be indicative of an emotional disturbance. However, fighting in a deprived area is a first, not a last, resort.

Possible Action: Check Tom's records for a history of previous emotional problems. If such a history exists refer him to the school social worker. If there is no history of emotional disturbance, talk with Tom and find the cause for the fights. Explain school rules against fighting on *school grounds.* (Don't tell him he shouldn't fight for this is probably foreign to his parent's advice. By necessity, a child must learn to take his part in a deprived area.) Offer your help and that of the guidance counselor and/or principal in helping settle his problems. Warn that future fights will bring some kind of penalty such as detention or a trip to the principal's office.

Informing Teachers of Available Help

If the new teacher knows he does not stand alone, he will walk through the classroom door with more confidence.

If time permits and specialists are available, each should be given the opportunity to give a brief talk explaining his role and how he can be contacted for help. A brief brochure or leaflet explaining services offered by school psychologists, social workers, counselors, remedial reading teachers and speech therapists is desirable for ready reference.

As the orientation nears its end each teacher is informed that this is only the beginning. In-service training in many areas will be provided throughout the year. Each teacher, on a regular basis, will be given the opportunity to observe master teachers at work.

After two or three days of intensive orientation the new teacher may be shaking his head in wonder. A normal reaction is: What am I doing here?

The last session should end on an informal, friendly note. For days the student has been discussed as an anonymous object of concern and future problems. There are any number of neighborhood children who would be delighted to be asked to join a soft drink and snack session with the new teachers. There is nothing like the friendliness of next week's students to dispel a great many unfounded concerns. The children, in turn, spread the word about the nice new teachers and opening day will be just a little easier.

The orientation is completed and the principal searches his mind for oversights. He gives every teacher a booklet of tips for opening week. He has made certain that all needed materials are stocked in every room. He gives his last bit of pre-school advice: "Relax this weekend. Go some place and enjoy yourselves."

Now every memorable minute of the first day belongs to the fledgling teacher. And that's the way it should be.

SUMMARY

The principal's success or failure depends, to a large degree, on his skill in human relations. The teacher is the key to a successful educational program and it is vital that no stone be left unturned in locating teacher talent. The alert principal identifies his vacancies as early as possible and sets up criteria for a replacement.

Teacher candidate interviews should be thorough. Basic attitudes vital to successful teaching in disadvantaged schools should be determined. Even with the beginning teacher, experience in working with deprived children should be sought.

Beginning teachers should be told the full facts about their school. Whitewashing is out, but at the same time misconceptions that all disadvantaged fit the same category should be dispelled.

Once the teachers have been hired the principal should help in getting them settled in the community and provide means of acquainting them with their teaching colleagues prior to school opening.

Intensive pre-school orientation is necessary to fully inform new teachers. In the opening sessions they should have school policies, regulations and the tenure process carefully explained.

In subsequent sessions they should be allowed to air their own concerns. A booklet of answers to anticipated questions does much to relieve these concerns.

A panel of experienced teachers is especially valuable in discussing common classroom problems, basic causes and possible action or solutions.

It is important for the new staff members to realize that specialists are available to help them with special problems. Orientation should include a thorough rundown of all special services.

Orientation should end on a friendly, informal note. The last session should include neighborhood children to provide a head start for establishing friendly relationships.

If the principal has done his job well, he has prepared the new staff for a momentous event — their first day as full-fledged teachers.

2

Working Effectively with Teachers
of the Disadvantaged

Teamwork is as essential on a school staff as it is on a winning football team. The principal's role can be compared to that of a quarterback. He calls the signals, but the other team members understand why and realize that their contributions are essential to the successful conclusion of the play.

The day of the autocratic principal is past and the pendulum has swung to a more militant teaching body that is demanding that its voice be heard and its opinions considered. This increased militancy has made the principal the "man in the middle." He has the unenviable task of carrying out the orders of his superiors, which are sometimes unpopular with his staff, while maintaining good relations with his teachers. There are times when it is impossible to please everyone. On these occasions, the principal's ability to function effectively depends upon diplomacy, toleration, compromise (not of principles but approaches), and how he has laid his teamwork foundations.

Cornerstones of this foundation are:

1. Teamwork must be based on mutual respect.
2. Teamwork must be based on the goal of providing children with the best education they are capable of achieving.
3. Teamwork depends upon full and open communication.
4. Teamwork must be practiced, not preached.

KEEPING TEACHERS INFORMED AND INVOLVED

Staff Bulletins

To insure fullest cooperation, every member of the team must be kept informed. Many elementary principals fall into the trap of believing that typically smaller elementary staffs are aware of what is happening without being told. They often learn differently when they find the teamwork approach blocked by misunderstandings.

Staff bulletins can be couriers of communication. They should tell the staff what is going on in school, who is doing it, and how things, in general, are progressing. In addition to the typical announcements of the coming week's events, space should be allotted for grade and room projects and curriculum activities. Teachers should be encouraged to contribute ideas and opinions for every issue. No opportunity should be missed to write of noteworthy activities of individual staff members.

Since weekly staff bulletins must be newsbriefs, periodic bulletins of a longer nature should be devoted to curriculum development activities, professional growth activities, and recognition of outstanding effort.

Bulletin boards in the teachers' workroom or lounge should not be overlooked as a means of communication. Activities and opportunities not ordinarily included in bulletins can be posted for dissemination.

Staff Meetings

High on most teachers' lists of necessary evils is the staff meeting. In general, they are considered a boring waste of time devoted to announcements and regulations that could be covered in a bulletin. Unfortunately, too often their criticisms are justified.

A staff meeting should involve, as the title indicates, the total staff and not consist of a principal's monologue of one way directives. When teachers feel they have an important part to play and can contribute their ideas and voice their concerns, objections to staff meetings are greatly lessened.

Fears of principals who have tried greater teacher participation have proved unfounded. One veteran principal remarked: "I'm going to try to involve my teachers, but I expect that most of the meetings will be short and sweet from now on."

He later admitted that most of his previous "clock watchers" had forgotten how to tell time.

The concern that only gripes and trivialities will be aired has also proved fallacious. The following topics were discussed by teachers at one school during monthly staff meetings.

The Disadvantaged Child—What's He Like? (geared primarily for new teachers on the staff)

The Role of the School Psychologist

Classroom Management (a panel discussion led by experienced teachers)

Aspects of the Nongraded School (lecture by college professor)

A staff discussion on school rules and regulations

A film viewing of a disadvantaged school followed by a discussion

Discussion and recommendations for purchase of playground equipment

A report on an upcoming science textbook adoption

The School Community Program (explained by the School Community Agent)

Planning of staff social affairs for the year

In encouraging total staff involvement, the principal must be prepared to find that on occasion staff ideas vary from his own. When this occurs, he should be willing to cooperate and work for a solution satisfactory to the majority. In the event the recommendations run counter to school district policies, the principal has the opportunity to explain the reasons for rejection. If the policy in question seems unreasonable or outmoded, the staff may wish to ask the Board for revision or amendment.

Grade Level Meetings

The principal of a disadvantaged school with his myriad duties and problems can't possibly become intimately acquainted with every subject in every grade. He must resign himself to the role of the instructional generalist and keep aware, through every possible means, of what is happening educationally at the various grade level meetings on a regular basis.

In addition to keeping abreast of what is happening in the classrooms, there are several other benefits that accrue. On a small group level the teacher and principal see the human side of each other. In discussing children and curriculum, they share common concerns. These meetings of mutual minds produce ideas which generate enthusiasm and lead to educational plans tailored to the needs of individual children.

In the grade level meeting, as in no other forum, the principal can get the teacher involved in active curriculum work. When the teacher is assured that his ideas are solicited and deemed worthy of consideration by the principal, he is willing to open up and answer questions that would otherwise be thought of as prying. The observations of experienced and successful teachers garnered from grade level meetings should be written down. They become valuable suggestions to pass on to new staff members.

Finding a time to conduct grade level meetings becomes a dilemma for the principal, especially if his staff is large. Meeting for about 30 minutes prior to school opening is usually acceptable and generally preferred to after school meetings. The best possible time is a luncheon meeting. Often it can be a brown bag lunch, with an occasional restaurant break. Aside from the advantage that lunch time is not thought of as an extra time encroachment, the relaxed atmosphere is conducive to sharing and working together.

The writer has found grade level meetings to be the single most effective method of working with his staff in bringing about curriculum changes.

Evaluation Committees

If the principal truly subscribes to the teamwork approach, he will not be content in asking the staff for new ideas in curriculum. He will go one step further and set up an evaluation committee. This requires total commitment because sacred cows cannot hide in the light of conscientious evaluation.

A typical curriculum evaluation report might reveal the following problem areas:

1. The instructional program is not geared to meet the individual needs of disadvantaged students.
2. Instructional materials do not meet the needs of the slower students.
3. The instructional program adheres too closely to the textbook.
4. Our students need more field trip experiences.
5. Class periods are too long for disadvantaged students.
6. There is not enough integration of subject matter; for example, art and social studies.
7. After-school programs are needed to keep our students off the streets.
8. Evening academic and recreational classes are needed for adults.

Evaluation committees should be established for all school areas. These committees could include:

1. School-Home Contacts

2. Playground
3. Student Health
4. School Citizenship
5. Race Relations
6. School-Social Agencies Relationships

Evaluation without follow-up is worthless. Recommendations should be carried out as quickly and completely as possible. It goes without saying that teachers should be involved in helping to bring about needed changes.

IN-SERVICE TRAINING

In-service education is often considered as only those days when school is dismissed for teacher instruction. The principal should consider in-service education as any program in which teacher growth is the purpose. With this in mind, almost any activity that involves teachers can be an opportunity for growth if it is well-planned and built around areas of teacher interest. Thus a pre-school or post-school conference can be as much an in-service experience as a workshop.

A good in-service program starts with the recognition of need by both adminstration and teachers.[1] Both must realize that changing educational needs and complex problems require new information and new solutions.

In recognizing the need for continuous education, the administration commits itself to released time for teachers and financial support.

The teacher commits himself to working toward solution of the problems selected and a willingness to work to stay abreast of sweeping educational advances.

Teachers must play a key part in planning in-service education. One workable plan is to appoint committees according to teacher interest and concern. One member from each committee becomes a part of a coordinating committee, which makes final selection and plans for areas that will be covered in a given year for the whole staff. The principal can also work with individuals on special problem areas not brought before the group.

Whether it be a one day workshop or a year long seminar, the selected problem should meet a perceived need of the teaching body. A survey is one of the best ways to arrive at teacher concerns. The surveys need not be complicated, as the following example attests.

[1] The Joint Committee on Conference and Curriculum Planning, *Evaluating the In-Service Education Program of Your Community School* (Lansing, Michigan: The Department of Public Instruction, 1957), p. 3.

Dear Teacher:

I am sure you are aware, by now, that our next in-service afternoon is on Friday, April 26.

Perhaps the following will be new information:

The afternoon session will be from 1:00 to 4:00 P.M.

After the sectional meetings, time has been set from 2:00 to 4:00 for district-wide grade level meetings.

The purpose of a grade level meeting is to exchange ideas and/or to talk about things of actual interest to the participants at the specific grade level.

Success of any meeting of this kind depends upon the involvement of those in the meeting. Will you help make the second grade meeting purposeful and valuable by taking a minute or two to indicate topics of interest to you or to indicate questions which would stimulate profitable discussion? Then we'll try to assemble the interests and structure the discussion around these interests.

LET'S MAKE THE SECOND GRADE MEETING WORTHWHILE!

- -

Please detach and return on or before Tuesday, March 19th.

TOPICS OR INTERESTS for discussion at the second grade meeting:

1. _____

2. _____

3. _____

4. _____

5. _____

_____   _____
Teacher   School

A survey may indicate a problem or interest area that requires more than a released day or two. In such instances workshops or seminars, both credit and non-credit, through cooperation with a college or university, can be set up to meet the need.

A questionnaire of twenty items at the writer's school indicated that a majority of the staff felt the graded organization was failing to meet the needs of the children. From this concern emerged a college credit course on the nongraded concept. The enthusiasm engendered by the course led to the decision to ungrade the first grade, with the rest of the grades to follow in subsequent years if the first grade experiment proved fruitful.

Evaluating In-Service Programs

A good in-service program cannot remain static. It must change to meet changes in personnel, the student body, and education. The in-service program should be analyzed periodically by both the principal and teachers to keep it meaningful and up-to-date. This can be accomplished by asking for written evaluations or through a prepared analysis scale. With either instrument, the respondent should have the choice of signing his name or remaining anonymous.

EVALUATING THE TEACHER'S PERFORMANCE

One of the biggest perils to a teamwork approach is teacher evaluations. When the principal is placed in the position of judging the teacher's performance, the relationship becomes something less than that of co-workers.

Despite the disadvantages, teacher evaluation is necessary. Tenure structure demands it. More importantly, teacher growth can be helped through a well-planned evaluative process.

The presence or absence of several factors will determine the success or failure of a teacher evaluation program.

The philosophy behind evaluation is of prime importance. The purpose of evaluation must be to stimulate self-improvement and help the teacher, with every possible resource, gain the improvement he seeks. If this philosophy is clearly understood by the staff, there is less resentment of observations. The majority of teachers will no longer consider classroom visitations as "snoopervising" but as a sincere effort to offer help when needed and praise when deserved. Of course, this feeling is strengthened if the principal has involved his staff in school affairs, considered their opinions, and worked as a team with them to help solve their problems.

A large measure of the evaluative process should be self-ratings by teachers. They should be encouraged to develop their own goals and establish some criteria for judging their success.

When teachers have a voice in rating their performance and can be assured that honest appraisals will bring efforts to help rather than criticism, there develops a willingness on the part of most to look at their teaching with an eye toward continued growth. Whatever rating instrument that is used should be teacher approved, if it is not developed by them. The rating scale should allow for a broad performance range. Otherwise, the unrealistic narrowness of "acceptable" or "unacceptable" or some similar term forces the teacher into an all or nothing appraisal. As one teacher observed: "You would have to be a fool to rate your methods as unacceptable. However, if a wide range of choices are present most teachers are willing to admit they're less than perfect."

Another form of evaluation aimed toward increased teacher effectiveness consists of a joint effort between the teacher and principal. Early in the year the principal and teacher, through a conference, establish areas of mutual agreement in which they wish to see improvement. The areas may cover a wide range of techniques and skills or be limited to one or two, such as better room control or development of more motivating instructional techniques. The teacher rates his daily performance. Two or three times a year the principal makes a formal observation which is followed by a conference. This approach creates a team effort toward a common goal and may develop a teacher attitude that evaluation is not only necessary but desirable.

Principals should make it clearly understood that evaluation is not two or three classroom visits, but the day-by-day performance that occurs throughout the year. Such an understanding allows for "bad" days which all teachers have, places a premium on consistent performance, and puts in proper perspective those teachers who have "prepared packages" for the principal's visits.

Every teacher has the right to know exactly what qualities and characteristics the principal considers most important. Since they too are very human (contrary to some teacher's opinions), principals have their own little quirks. Some things that loom large on their horizons are distinctly smaller for the teacher. Thus, if noise in the halls is a principal's pet peeve, every teacher should know this fact.

The principal who wants to compare his philosophy with his staff and who sincerely wants to check his own performance will ask the teachers to evaluate him. For the sake of objectivity, teachers should not be asked to sign their names. These evaluations should be considered in the same light as those given the teachers. If growth in certain areas is needed, it should be actively pursued.

After the Evaluation What?

The check-list observation form has come under heavy fire from teachers. Certainly it can be regarded as no more than a springboard for a conference that will follow an observation.

More refined methods of observations are being used in many schools. Tape recordings of teaching sessions allow the teacher to analyze his teaching style.

Motion pictures, filmstrips, tapes and video tapes of effective teaching methods are becoming readily available to principals. These can be used with the total staff or individual teachers to help bring about desired change.

If a teacher, new or experienced, is doing less than an adequate job of teaching, the principal should use every possible resource to help. Opportunities to observe demonstration teaching, visits to the classrooms of highly capable teachers, new sources of materials, the help of a "buddy" teacher, plus the friendly guidance of the principal should be given without reservation and as often as needed.

If All Else Fails, Then What?

Not every person who enters the profession has the ability to become a good teacher. This is a fact that everyone knows but few accept. Teachers protest at unfavorable evaluations and often refuse to accept the fact that they aren't working out. Principals hesitate to "turn thumbs down" on a teacher after he has spent years preparing for the profession. As a result, many teachers who are inadequate are granted tenure on the rationalization that they will improve with experience. Principals with any experience as a gauge know that if a teacher is doing less than a satisfactory job after two or three years of probation, his chances of radically improving are very slight.

The principal's ultimate loyalty is to the 25 or more students that will be exposed to the teacher year after year. If he has serious doubts about what will happen to those students, it is his duty, no matter how painful, to try to counsel him to enter another profession.

The demands are greater for those who would teach the disadvantaged. The principal has to be wary of those aflame with the missionary spirit, who consider teaching the deprived as some sort of crusade, but have little real understanding or empathy for those they would "save." This is not to downgrade dedication and zeal, but the daily trials of dealing with the myriad problems of the deprived takes understanding of children as they are, and working with them from that point. Success comes slowly and in small doses, a fact which often causes the first blushes of zeal to fade, with nothing to take its place.

Many teachers fail in the disadvantaged school because they simply can't overcome their middle-class backgrounds and ideals. In this case, if potential exists, the teacher should be counseled to try a school in which the students' backgrounds are similar to his own.

Mrs. X is a good example. Her statements graphically illustrate the anguish suffered by a misassigned teacher.

"I've nearly reached the end of my rope. The kids disturb me so much I can't sleep or eat.

"I can't even enjoy my weekends without worrying about all those troublemakers in my class."

Despite her problems with the disadvantaged, Mrs. X showed many promising qualities. She was discouraged and ready to give up teaching. She finally agreed to try a middle-class school in another town and adjusted with good success. A month or so after her move a letter was received which began:

"Thanks for being an understanding principal. Things are working out fine in my new school. I realize now that some teachers are better suited to certain kinds of children. I feel much better about myself and my teaching since I've learned that fact."

On the other hand, there are those whose shortcomings look like a treatise on how not to teach. There was Mr. Y as a case in point. Observations revealed the following reasons why Mr. Y was obviously not cut out for teaching.

1. Students out of their seats without permission and wandering around the room for no reason.
2. Students talking across the room to each other.
3. Students shouting down the teacher when he tried to instruct them.
4. Students fighting in the classroom, throwing paper wads, pulling hair and tripping.
5. No lesson plans or definite organization for subject instruction.
6. Practically nothing in the way of motivating material.
7. Practically all lecture and very little active learning experiences for the children.

Despite all the help that was given, Mr. Y failed to improve. He had no rapport with the youngsters and they had no respect for him. Mr. Y resigned when he learned his release was imminent and decided to give up teaching for sales work.

KEEPING TEACHER MORALE HIGH

A principal of the writer's acquaintance once asked why I thought he had such a large staff turnover each year.

He was known as a perfectionist who was quick to criticize and slow to praise. When I suggested that perhaps a few more compliments and recognition for jobs well done might help, he replied: "I consider all my teachers professionals. If I don't say anything to them, I am pleased with their work."

My rejoinder was: "They may be professionals, but they're human beings first and foremost. If they're doing a good job, they want to hear it from you."

"Give them the roses while they work" philosophy can create a climate conducive to cooperation, congeniality, innovation and dedication. The teacher of the disadvantaged has more than his share of worries, frustrations and heartaches. If he feels his principal knows, cares and appreciates, the problems become a little easier to bear.

Keep an "Open Door" and "Open Ear" Policy

Every principal needs to learn a basic skill taught in kindergarten and first grade. *Learn to listen.* Often there are problems without solution and the teacher knows it. But the opportunity to talk about it to someone who understands may keep the teacher from becoming discouraged and throwing up his hands in resignation.

An open door encourages communication. Closed doors are barriers that can send teachers home to brood and worry when a few minutes of listening time could have solved the problem, or at least helped.

The wise principal puts the human side—staff, pupils and parents—ahead of paper work, salesmen and all the administrative trivia connected with the principalship. Time can always be found for paper work, but often a personnel problem must be handled at the exact time it arises.

Cultivate Good Will

Standing in the outer office in the morning to say "hello" and in the afternoon to say "goodnight" indicates friendly interest and pays off in good will.

A note of thanks for some extra effort takes little time but can be the incentive for many such efforts during the year. One teacher prized these so highly, her daughter informed me, that she kept a special scrapbook for complimentary and thank-you notes received from the principal.

Not everyone appreciates a birthday, but he appreciates recognition when it occurs. It is a simple matter to compile a list of all staff birthdays and send each a birthday card as they occur.

One surprised recipient, after receiving a card, remarked: "I've been teaching fifteen years and this is the nicest recognition a principal ever gave me."

Extraordinary achievement should be rewarded with special recognition. Certificates of appreciation for outstanding achievement at a year end dinner or party makes a memorable occasion for recipients.

Retiring teachers, who have given long years of service, should not go unnoticed. A retirement dinner, attended by the whole staff, can become the highlight of the school social year. Retirees appreciate such affairs when they are kept on a light note and do not become overly sentimental or emotional.

Good Working Conditions Contribute to Good Morale

Little irritants which may seem unimportant to the principal can affect a teacher's outlook toward his job. A majority of elementary teachers are women who have little knack for repairing or adding the small physical trappings that make working conditions better or more pleasant. There should be a clear policy that a custodian or custodians are available to help with loose hinges, balky windows, dull pencil sharpeners, and all the other small tasks that must be done in every school, every day.

A pleasant, spacious teachers' workroom or lounge, neatly kept and comfortably furnished, adds much to teacher morale. It should contain a telephone, coffee and pop machines, and several educational magazines. Professional books can also be kept in the lounge. If the school budget does not allow for an adequate professional library, staff members are often willing to contribute their own on a loan basis.

Planning for Play

One of the first orders of business each school year should be the formation of a social committee. A well-planned slate of activities can do much to keep spirits high. Included in these activities can be picnics and pot-luck dinners, as well as other fun sessions of a more formal nature.

Staff recreation such as bowling and volleyball should be planned and encouraged. Evening activities of a family nature are welcomed by married staff members.

If the faculty has a large number of new teachers, the principal can assist in forming a Newcomers' Club. Activities can be planned to acquaint members with each other and their new community. There is an educational bonus in a Newcomers' Club. Members, especially new teachers, find they are sharing many similar beginning problems. This realization dispels fears and doubts and makes adjustment easier.

Does It Pay to Play?

There may be reasonable doubts about the strong emphasis on social activities and play. An equally reasonable question might be: Is it worth all the effort? The answer is: Yes, yes, a thousand times yes.

If there is a good feeling among staff members and between the staff and principal, out of the ordinary requests become favors gladly granted and burdens not grumbled about.

In an atmosphere of good feeling the principal becomes liked as well as respected. Like the teacher who kept a scrap book of a principal's notes, he might be able to start one of his own with teacher notes like the example below.

Dear Mr. Principal,

Your kindness, interest and friendliness has been a tremendous source of encouragement and inspiration to me as I am sure it has to many others.

Mary Doe

SUMMARY

The successful principal operates his school through a teamwork approach. This approach is gained through mutual respect, full and open communication, and is based on providing the best possible education for children.

The teamwork approach demands that teachers be kept informed and involved. Staff bulletins should serve as forums for teacher ideas and keep the staff informed of noteworthy activities in various classrooms. Staff meetings should involve the total staff. This can be accomplished by establishing committees for various school areas and allowing teachers to serve on committees of interest.

There are many benefits to be derived from grade level meetings. They are an effective means of bringing about curriculum change.

Evaluation committees, composed of teachers, can bring to light needed changes in curriculum and other school areas.

Any program designed to bring about teacher growth should be considered in-service training. Both principals and teachers play an important part in planning in-service education. Surveys are helpful in arriving at needed programs. Evaluations should be an integral part of in-service programs.

Self-improvement should be a prime purpose of teacher evaluations and self-ratings should play an important part. Evaluations should be based on day-by-day performance and not solely on one or two formal teaching observations. Evaluation should not be a one way street. Principals conscientious about their own performance should request teacher evaluations.

When a teacher is encountering problems, it is the principal's obligation to offer all possible help. If all efforts fail, the principal's ultimate loyalty is to the students and it is his duty to deny continued employment.

Teacher morale is an important factor in the successful operation of a school. Recognition and praise for good work, listening sympathetically to teacher problems, and exhibiting friendliness all pay off in good will.

Pleasant working conditions and a well-planned schedule of several social activities are sure-fire morale builders.

Is it worth it? This is a legitimate question a principal must ask about any administrative endeavor. In the case of efforts directed toward keeping teacher morale high, the answer will be an unqualified *yes.*

3

Solving Problems with Parents, Pupils, and Staff Members

The disadvantaged school offers a principal more problems of greater magnitude than those encountered in middle-class settings. Indeed, unless the principal has workable solutions to the seemingly endless problems that come across his desk he is in danger of being overwhelmed by sheer numbers.

How a principal handles "people problems"—whether it be his custodial staff or dealing with a council of parents—determines how he will be regarded by those with whom and for whom he works.

There is no one approach that is equally effective in working with everyone. People are as varied as their problems. However, there are several underlying factors that are the bases of workable solutions. It goes without saying that fairness, honesty and truthfulness must be present in any decision making. In addition, there should be a complete understanding of the position of all participants involved. Finally, when some agreed plan is reached there must be trust that each party will carry out his part.

UNUSUAL PUPIL PROBLEMS

In September the principal of a disadvantaged school must expect to encounter stealing, lying, cheating, fighting, truancy, extortion, teacher defiance and refusal to work on a regular basis. Ways of dealing with these are discussed in Chapter 9.

The less frequent, but more severe problems, are dilemmas that lead to sleepless nights and add worry wrinkles. Sooner or later cases similar to the following will present themselves for the principal's attention:

- The battered child who explains: "My dad got mad and beat me with his fists."
- The girl who states: "My stepfather (or some other adult) is getting 'dirty' with me."
- The pre-teen girl who is having sexual relations with older boys and/or older adults.
- The mother who is spending A.D.C. money on neighborhood men.
- The mother who practices prostitution in her home.
- The parent who neglects his children's most basic needs.

Talking to parents is usually not effective in these extreme cases. In some instances, it can make the situation even worse for the child, a fact the principal should keep uppermost in mind when contemplating this tack.

The importance of the principal's close working cooperation with other community agencies has been pointed out in other chapters. If this exists, investigation and "pressure" can be brought to bear when involved families have some connection with these agencies, which is often the case.

There are cases when nothing short of legal means will remedy the situation. State laws exist for the protection of children. The fact that court action can be unpleasant should not deter the principal. The writer has been threatened on several occasions for "poking his nose in where he had no business." To this date, though, a threat has never been carried out. Adults who abuse or neglect children rarely have the courage to face up to "righteous anger."

WORKING WITH UNCOOPERATIVE PARENTS

By and large, parents in a deprived area will work with the school when they are asked to help with their children's problems. Often what appears to be uncooperative behavior is due to misunderstanding. As an example, a teacher who requested that girls remove their heavy, fur-lined boots in the class-room received an angry note from the parent stating: "My daughter can wear her boots any place she wants." When she understood the request was made for health reasons, her attitude completely changed.

There are reasons for regulations, and making certain that these reasons are well-known by pupils and parents alike can clear up many areas of misunderstanding.

Parents of poor children are quick to complain about treatment they consider "unfair" to their children. Perhaps due to some of their own unhappy school experiences, many rely on their children's version of an incident without asking for the teacher's explanation and respond with angry notes or telephone calls.

Responding to an angry note with a friendly, explanatory letter is often effective. An invitation for a conference, or where the teacher is willing, an observation of the class at work, gives the parent the opportunity to make first-hand judgments.

Emotional, often abusive, telephone calls can result from a child's school problem. The most effective technique for handling this problem is to *listen.* Trying to interrupt or becoming angry only worsens the situation. After the parent has had his full say, he is willing to listen. In fact, when he calms down he is often ashamed of his outburst and becomes agreeable to almost any reasonable suggestion.

Problems Associated with Parent Help

Some parents who are willing to work with the school see corporal punishment as the only solution to misbehavior. The writer has often encountered parents who couldn't understand why this method was not applied to all—boys *and* girls—for the slightest infraction. Indeed, parental fixation on this subject can close the avenues between home and school. A principal or teacher is unwilling to contact the home about problems if they result in beatings.

When this thinking prevails in the home, every means of counseling should be used to point out other more desirable and effective ways of child control.

On the other hand, there are some parents who reject the idea that school authorities have any control over their children's behavior. They insist that they be contacted "when my child gets out of line." The fact that this is often impractical and time-consuming for minor matters is usually not enough to change their determined stand. In this situation, the principal has two alternatives. He can follow the parents' suggestions and call them repeatedly. After a time, parents have been known to change their stand when their daily routine was constantly interrupted. The other approach is to point out that the school has basic responsibilities and concomitant controls necessary to carry out those responsibilities. Remaining firm in this insistence usually gets results with the passing of time. In one instance, a father who had a reputation for coming to school and "telling off" teachers and principals was confronted on a couple of occasions with a no-nonsense approach that included some possible consequences of his actions. He later became a contributing member to the local parent organization.

The apathetic and passive parent approach is the most common and frustrating of all to the principal. The parent listens and appears interested in effecting a solution. Despite this show of cooperativeness, there is no follow through on any plan of action. In cases such as these it is worth the time and effort to work patiently to gain parent effort. However, after a time, the situation must be faced realistically and the principal must look for solutions that do not depend on parent help.

WORKING WITH NON-TEACHING PERSONNEL

In arriving at priorities, the teachers should occupy the greater share of the principal's attention. However, other building personnel, secretaries, custodians, cooks and bus drivers, must come in for their share of his concern. Though playing a different role, if they are made to feel a part of the educational team and sound personnel practices are instituted in working with them, a smoother functioning unit will result.

Principal-Secretary Relationship

A good secretary makes her boss a more effective school leader. In a deprived school, the principal's office is the hub of constant activity. In the midst of this, the secretary must keep her composure, become a storehouse of school knowledge, and know how to separate the significant from the insignificant in order to make certain that her boss's time is not consumed with trivialities.

The good secretary in a deprived school must possess all the characteristics of a good secretary in any setting – and more. Important is the liking for and understanding of poor children. Without it she will not be able to exercise patience in her many contacts with them. Organizational ability must be a strong point for the office must function smoothly though dealing with pupils and parents who often exemplify disorganization.

To achieve peak efficiency, there must be a loyalty and working closeness between secretary and principal. While the secretary should be made to feel a valued member, the office should not become a forum for her personal problems. One principal, who started listening sympathetically to the home problems his secretary's teenage daughter was creating, found a good hour of his daily time usurped listening to her family woes.

"When I finally told her I couldn't devote so much time to non-school problems, she became upset," he recounted. "I realized too late that I should have made this clear the first time the matter came up."

Working Harmoniously with the Custodial Staff

Stories of eccentric custodians are almost as prevalent as traveling salesmen jokes. Almost every school, it seems, has, at some time in its history, had a janitor who marched to his own music and felt his authority to be at least equal to the principal's. Ancient school history can be funny but it is no laughing matter when teachers and custodians are conducting a running feud.

Instilling pride of performance and a concern for the appearance of the school should be every principal's aim. Complimenting good work is one sure way to get repeat performances. A periodic building check that concentrates as much on the positive as areas of concern indicates to the custodial staff that the principal is aware of their efforts.

Monthly meetings make the custodians feel a part of the building team. This is an excellent forum for clearing up misunderstandings. When a janitor understands the reason for a work creating seating arrangement, he may be less inclined to grumble at the inconvenience. These meetings often spawn excellent suggestions of educational value. For example, a "Cleanest Room Award" was the brain child of one custodian who also purchased a banner which was displayed in the winning room for a week. Children worked hard to win the prized banner and developed neater work habits in the process.

Custodian concerns should not dictate teaching styles, but their opinions should be considered by the teachers. Room arrangement is often an important factor in effective teaching and teachers should be encouraged to try various seating plans. However, unusual seating arrangements with no educational thought that create extra custodial work should be discouraged. Crayons and pencils lying on the floor create hazards. In addition, crushed crayons grind into the floor and cause custodians to grind their teeth. Custodians appreciate a room clean-up by pupils prior to school dismissal.

Custodians are often sensitive and resent being "bossed around" by teachers. One janitor indicated this in his appraisal of a staff member. "She acts like she is Miss High and Mighty and tries to tell me what to do. I take my orders from my supervisors, not her." To prevent this sort of clash, it should be clearly understood by all staff members — teachers and custodians alike — that custodian orders come through the principal and head custodian, if there is one so designated.

Teacher requests for special custodial service should be written on forms provided for that purpose and require the principal's signature. This system allows the custodial staff to plan their work and better utilize their time.

"Otherwise," as one custodian noted, "you can't step out in the hall without three different teachers wanting you to do three different things at once."

A spat between a teacher and a custodian should not be allowed to smolder. It's true that some teachers are untidy and some janitors lazy. More often accusations such as these stem from misunderstandings. Usually the principal can ease the friction with no hard feelings.

Occasionally a shift of a custodian to another room may be necessary when a personality confict arises.

Work schedules, listing shift tasks and times assigned to each, are desirable for many reasons. They help the principal and head custodian equalize work loads and forestall complaints of "I do more work than so and so." The schedule, at a glance, establishes accountability and prevents blanket criticism when only one person is falling down in his work; and when illness strikes, a ready plan exists for substitutes.

Regular building checks should be a part of the head custodian's duties. Janitors should know in advance what areas are being checked. Indeed, encouraging each to carry a check-list with him on his rounds can result in self-evaluation, the best route to a clean building.

Handling Transportation Problems

When something goes wrong with the transportation system, the principal can expect an avalanche of parent protests. When possible, he should ask to be included in assignment of bus drivers serving his school and selection of student loading zones.

The same qualities of patience, calmness, understanding, firmness and consistency that make for successful teacher-pupil relationships are essential also for a driver.

Student loading zones present a particular problem in congested and/or industrial areas typical of deprived neighborhoods. One of the best ways of establishing pick-up points is to drive the area at times when the children will embark and debark. Using this approach allows better identification of trouble and hazardous areas. For example, streets near a factory that are quiet and lightly traveled during most of the day may be crowded with traffic around 8:00 A.M. and 4:00 P.M., the same times when children are being transported to and from school. Generally pick-up points should not be located near:

- Bars and poolrooms (young children should not be deliberately exposed to toughs and drunks)
- Railroad tracks and marshalling yards
- Abandoned houses
- Factory entrances
- Stores (the temptation of goods for which there is no money can encourage stealing)

The first step to minimizing bus problems is to expect that they will arise. Definite rules should be established and made clear to pupils, parents and bus drivers. These may be included in student and parent handbooks or handled as separate fliers. The emphasis that all regulations arise out of a concern for the pupils' safety leaves little sound argument on either the pupils' or parents' part when infractions occur.

If problems are handled early in the year in a no-nonsense manner, they may prevent an increasing build-up as the year progresses. Drivers should be encouraged to report infractions early and not wait until they become serious or widespread. At the first infraction, a letter stating the problem should go home to the parent. The letter should clearly emphasize that the child will not be allowed to jeopardize the safety of himself and others. The parents' cooperation should be solicited. A duplicate copy of the letter should be placed on file.

In the cases where continued infractions occur, temporary riding suspension may have to be invoked. A clearly outlined procedure of suspension, preferably drawn up by the Board of Education, should spell out reasons for suspension, the length of suspension time, and who has the authority to suspend. Based on years of experience, it is the writer's opinion that bus drivers should not be allowed suspension powers. Often, caught up in the emotion of the moment, rash sentences are invoked, for which the principal is expected to answer. It is hard to defend such acts as three day suspensions for throwing a paper wad on the floor. On the other hand, in extreme cases the driver should be allowed to eject students from the bus for one day only, provided he notifies the principal at the earliest possible moment.

When suspension becomes necessary, the parent should receive full details. A telephone message, followed by a confirming letter, has been the most successful approach for the writer.

As in all areas of school relations, the positive should be promoted. Some drivers are able to build esprit de corp and cooperation through a "safest bus" competition with other buses. The competition, based on a weekly or bi-weekly period, has at stake a school banner which resides in the winning bus. Other techniques as varied as "Safe Rider" buttons or taped music, jokes and riddles for replay on a portable tape recorder have proved successful in some cases.

The principal should encourage any ideas that offer the possibilities of making the wheels (pun intended) roll more smoothly.

WORKING WITH TEACHERS' PROBLEMS AND PROBLEM TEACHERS

Teachers are prone to human frailties (as are principals) and the principal can expect that some of these weaknesses will bring him anxious moments at some time or other during the year.

Showing a friendly concern for teachers as persons and treating them in a professional manner will minimize many trouble spots, but it will not completely eliminate such problems as the following.

Uncooperative Teachers

Lack of cooperation takes many forms and is one of the hardest problems to combat. Usually it is subtle rather than overt and the person practicing it can find wholesale rationalizations for doing so.

The teacher who insists on going his own way creates a further problem of resentment on the part of staff members who comply with school policies and procedures.

When the principal ignores obvious cases of uncooperative behavior, he faces the double danger of loss of respect of other staff members and defection of some who say "if so and so can do what he wants so can I."

When the principal encounters lack of cooperation, he should try to establish the reasons for it. Among the questions he might ask himself are:

- Am I asking for performance the teacher (s) is incapable of doing?
- If possible, has the teacher (s) been involved in the decision in question?
- Does the teacher (s) fully understand the reasons for the change and how to perform it?

- Does this way show promise of being better than the old or a different way?
- Are children likely to benefit more from this approach?
- If I were a teacher, would I resent following this approach?

If close examination reveals no good educational reason for failure to cooperate, a conference should be arranged with the teacher(s) in question. Handling the problem diplomatically and appealing to professional pride may be sufficient to bring about desired change. This first meeting should include reiteration of the reasons and benefits of preferred procedure, the importance of the teacher's role in the process, and a request for teacher suggestions that might be incorporated in the plan. Typed minutes of the conference give importance to the meeting as well as recording suggestions, concessions and other pertinent matters.

If lack of cooperation continues, a second conference, firmer in direction, will become necessary. At this time possible administrative action can be outlined.

In some cases, satisfactory decisions are never effected. At this juncture, the principal should start to document, making certain the teacher receives a copy, incidents or behavior he cannot overlook. When this point is reached, both principal and teacher will probably be agreeable to an end-of-year transfer.

Asking a teacher who refuses to cooperate to leave may appear to be an unsuccessful solution. However, in the final analysis it is better than a constant running battle or complete acquiescence for the sake of harmony. Could any principal call himself a leader if he occupied the following position?

A school visitor, on meeting a staff member in the hall, inquired: "Where may I find the office of the school leader?"

"If you are looking for the principal," he was informed, "his office is down the hall. If you want the person who is running the school, you will find her classroom just around the corner."

Dealing with Tongue Trouble

A college degree can add polish but it has little effect on basic human nature. Within the ranks of teachers are those who gossip, make unjustified accusations and lie.

Gossip can divide a staff and destroy close cooperation when it is directed toward members of the staff. It becomes a serious breach of ethics when it involves pupils and parents.

Accusations can seriously undermine the efforts of the principal or staff members. The principal should know the difference between honest, working complaints and harmful talk. If it exceeds the bounds of good taste he can expect to hear of it from concerned teachers or from the aggrieved subject of the talk.

An opening move to this situation can be a frank discussion of the matter in a staff meeting. Another recourse is private talks with the talking party(ies). More drastic measures are conferences involving the complainant, defendant and principal. A last resort is the referral of a case to an Ethics Committee of teachers. Understandably, this action is distasteful to everyone involved. However, it is preferable to unbridled tongues which rent a school staff and cause transfers, block educational team work, and harm school-community relations.

Handling "Hot-Heads"

High-tempered staff members pose a special problem. They are usually energetic, hard-working and concerned teachers who perform well until someone or something sets off an explosion. Such an outburst can trigger a slap or some other unacceptable form of pupil discipline or "telling off" a colleague or parent.

Any incidents of this nature should result in a conference with the teacher in question. Counseling should build on teacher strengths and suggest alternate approaches to behavior and incidents that trigger extreme action. In many cases the security afforded by the principal's confidence and development of techniques for handling anger-provoking situations help lower the boiling point. In those instances when little improvement results despite an honest effort on the teacher's part, the principal can suggest a physical examination to determine if the cause might be attributable to a nervous or other physical condition. A recommendation for psychiatric treatment might also appear necessary.

"Let us reason together" is a good philosophy for the principal who daily faces a potpourri of problems. A conference built on helpful counseling may be sufficient to correct the teacher who arrives late for school, who leaves classes unsupervised or uses sick leave inappropriately. When problems persist, it is apparent that the principal tried and that subsequent action was caused by teacher failure — not administrative indifference.

Some Problem Areas to Avoid

The principal is expected to be competent in the field of education.

His training does not include finance, psychiatry or law, to name a few. Yet in the course of the year he may be asked for advice in all these areas and others by anxious or troubled teachers. As flattering as their confidence may be, the principal should shy away from offering recommendations where expert advice is needed.

The teacher on the verge of bankruptcy or alcoholism needs the soundest advice available. The principal can help most by steering him to a reliable source of aid.

People with marital troubles seek the comfort of a sympathetic ear. While some principals argue that anything troubling a teacher affects classroom performance and thus is within the realm of the principal's concern, many pitfalls abound when assuming the role of the marriage counselor.

First, the principal hears only one side of the story. Second, the other marriage partner may rightfully assume it is none of the principal's business. Third, under the stress of emotion, the principal may hear intimate details that will become a source of embarrassment to the teacher if the rift is healed. Finally, if the teacher is a female and divorce ensues, there is always the possibility that mere concern may be misconstrued, and the principal may find himself in the delicate position of trying to escape unwanted attentions.

The principal's day is crowded and good administration demands that he constantly make priority judgments. In light of this, one must wonder if time spent directly on educational matters would not prove to be more beneficial to the total student body than hours devoted to personal problems for which he has neither the training nor knowledge.

"Last Straw" Measures

At some time in his career every principal will face teachers who have no business in education. The teacher may be incompetent in any of a number of ways. Despite the fact that a great debate rages whether an administrator possesses the necessary skills to evaluate a teacher's performance as good or bad, a poor teacher stands out like a flag in a strong breeze. Deprived children need the best teachers. No one likes to say "you won't do" to a person who has spent four college years preparing for a career. But the pupils' welfare must rank first with the principal and he is not acting professionally if he allows an incompetent teacher to gain tenure status.

On occasion, irresponsible and even unprincipled people enter teaching. They have no deep and lasting commitment to education, treating it as an unpleasant duty necessary for earning a living and/or as a happy hunting ground for their own personal pleasure and gain. The pupil never comes first in their thoughts and efforts and rarely is their second best adequate to meet pupil needs. The principal should entertain no doubts in denying tenure to those who treat teaching in this manner.

Unfortunately, principals often inherit someone else's mistakes in judgment. The tenure teacher who has turned sour or has become ineffective and unproductive poses the toughest problem of all. Tenure, with its admirable purpose of offering job security, also serves to protect the incompetent and unworthy. Even in extreme cases, when all forms of local administrative pressure fail to bring a resignation, there is a hesitancy to force a tenure trial. Past history has shown that teachers win far more often than Boards of Education when this final step is taken. Quite often the case is lost on a legal technicality rather than the main issue at hand.

The principal who decides his only recourse lies in the release of a tenure teacher should hold frequent conferences and offer all possible help to improve the situation. While such offers are usually spurned or unsuccessful with a teacher who has spent years on the job, the principal, like the captain of a ship, should first try to save before abandoning. This effort also becomes important to tenure board members who will make the final decision. All conference minutes, recommendations, observations and reports of unprofessional action should be carefully documented and dated, with one copy going to the teacher.

Members of the local teachers' organization should be involved. These representatives serve the twofold purpose of advising and aiding the teacher in question. At the same time, they have the opportunity to make first-hand observations and reach a professional decision accordingly to support the teacher or Board of Education. Finally, legal counsel for the school should advise the principal and Board on proper procedures and handle all technical matters pertaining to the law.

As unpleasant as some personnel problems can be, the principal should not lose sight of the fact that most people—pupils, parents and teachers—never constitute real trouble for him. That thought should keep him reasonably optimistic about his present program and future plans.

SUMMARY

Personnel problems must rank number one on the principal's priority list.

Pupil problems with their source in the home present some of the most worrisome dilemmas. Solutions may range from contact with other social agencies to court action.

Problems with parents often occur due to misunderstanding school regulations and procedures. Explanations through letters, telephone calls and conferences are means that should be used extensively to bring about better cooperation.

Non-teaching personnel should be made to feel a part of the educational team. Sound personnel policies are just as important for secretaries, custodians, cooks and bus drivers as they are for teachers.

Transportation, a special concern of parents, should receive careful attention from the principal. Establishing safe student loading locations and developing a system for regulating transportation safety can forestall many future situations.

Talking things through should be the first step in dealing with uncooperative or unprofessional teachers. There are some areas the principal is not equipped to handle. When asked for advice on money, marital or mental problems, the best help is to steer troubled teachers to professionals trained in these areas.

The difficult decision of denying tenure should not be shunned if it becomes necessary. Releasing a teacher with tenure status, perhaps the most time-consuming and difficult personnel problem of all, should, in good professional conscience, be initiated when all efforts to improve performance are rejected or fruitless and the children's educational interests are being harmed.

4

Meeting Special Needs
of Disadvantaged Students

The deprived child is a paradox to many who teach him. Countless pamphlets, articles and volumes have described his language deficiencies, his health, social and emotional needs, his anti-school attitude, rebellious behavior and all the rest of the syndrome. Unfortunately, for many the description is all too accurate. On the other hand the disadvantaged child is basically no different from his middle-class peers in that he wants acceptance, to feel good about himself, success, praise, and to like and be liked. Successful teaching in the disadvantaged school lies in using these strong human needs as a springboard to learning.

To those who face the awesome task of educating their charges to overcome their improverished background, the task sometimes appears overwhelming. As one teacher put it: "You need the wisdom of Solomon, the patience of Job, and the strength and endurance of Samson."

No doubt all these attributes are of great help, but far less ordinary teachers have found the keys to stimulate, to plant ambition, and to instill knowledge that unlocked the doors of poverty and all its accompanying woes.

The keys that unlock the doors are understanding of the child and his world, acceptance of him and his attitudes, and offering help and approaches geared to his abilities and special needs.

All aspects of the disadvantaged student's life must be considered in educating him. His nutrition is of prime importance for education will not take place on an empty belly. His health is of vital concern for an aching tooth can make the adventures of Rover and Susie seem totally unimportant. Ragged clothes can make him ashamed to attend and keep him away from school. His emotional state cannot be overlooked for a family fight or other troubles can send him to school distraught, angry, rebellious and aggressive.

The manifold ills of the "typical" deprived neighborhood and the needs of the "typical" disadvantaged child have been studied extensively in professional literature. The informed principal will have read much of this literature but he will not automatically assume that his students are typical. There are degrees of deprivation although most of the literature deals only with inner-city, hard-core poverty. Many suburban areas have slum districts in which the inhabitants would range somewhere near the middle of a continuum between middle class and hard-core poverty. These children have deficits to a lesser degree than their big city peers but lack many of the advantages of the middle class.

There are also degrees of deprivation within a disadvantaged neighborhood. Some families are quite prosperous and stress middle-class values but remain within the blighted neighborhood by choice, or more often because other areas are closed to them.

Gaining Information Through Surveys

Surveys of students, teachers and parents are fairly simple means to arrive at attitudes, perceptions and needs of children within a particular school.

It goes without saying that some kinds of educational decisions and action will be based on results of the surveys. Without this course of action, there is no real answer to the resentment of some who may regard surveys as prying and intrusions on their privacy.

Home Environment Surveys

Home environment factors have a great influence on the child's learning. Parental support and interest in the child's learning do much to shape his attitudes toward school and education.

Does anyone look at your report card? Does anyone help you with your school work? Questions such as these can be quite revealing indicators of parent supportiveness.

To a certain extent school readiness is helped by culture expanding media. Responses to questions of whether a child's home receives a newspaper, whether they read the newspaper, whether they have books and magazines in the home, and whether they read books at home for pleasure all have educational implications for the principal and his staff.

Most middle-class parents believe that giving the child jobs to do at home helps develop social responsibility. Merely asking students whether they have jobs to do at home will reveal to some degree the effort parents are making to develop responsibility.

It has often been stated that the child is the product of his environment. He is shaped and molded by his home and neighborhood surroundings and conditions. The school must attempt to negate, when possible, the self-defeating forces that are influencing him.

Sweeping panaceas will not be found. The myriad problems that affect the disadvantaged must be attacked in equally myriad ways. Success comes slowly and sometimes not at all. But any approach that offers some hope of alleviation or correction is better than no attempt at all.

Thus, if the results of a survey indicate an overwhelming lack of newspapers, magazines and books in the home, there are ways to provide them.

Newspaper publishers are usually willing to provide unsold papers free of cost for class and home use. Book stores and newsstands usually are given credit for unsold magazines by tearing off the front covers and returning them to the publishers.

The magazines, minus covers, are just as effective for school and home reading. Due to lack of storage space, many libraries are destroying older issues of magazines. Back issues of *National Geographic, Life, Look* and other publications heavily loaded with pictures have built-in motivation for reluctant readers.

Church and social groups readily conduct magazine drives when requested, and service organizations often provide funds to buy paperbacks for use in disadvantaged areas.

Newspapers and magazines can be used in dozens of ways on every grade level. The principal and his staff should develop suggestions and guidelines for using these current and colorful media in classroom instruction.

Knowledge of home conditions and degree of parent support should be factors in determining homework policies. If home conditions are crowded and noisy, with no suitable place or time provided for study, homework has little educational value and places one more pressure on the child. If a parent feels, as one child reported to her teacher, "You tell that teacher to stop wasting your time with that foolishness," there is little hope that homework will provide its intended independent learning experiences.

In general, it is safe to state that conditions in deprived areas are not conducive to extensive homework. The major homework values of learning to work independently, planning time for assigned tasks, and applying recent classroom learning can be best provided in the school setting.

Family Health Surveys

Principals and teachers are aware that hungry, sick, and sleepy children cannot learn effectively. The worst cases of health neglect are easily spotted. However, the extent of neglect in the total school population is easily overlooked. Family health surveys, taken during health classes, can give a picture of the eating and sleeping habits of children and the medical and dental attention they receive.

"Do you eat breakfast every morning?" is a question that can elicit a response that even shocks long-time teachers of the disadvantaged.

Another eye-opener is the fact that a great number of school children cook their own meals. One survey of 700 elementary school children revealed that 69 percent cooked at least one meal each day.[1]

Sleeping conditions and habits provide answers for the many listless, tired children who often fall asleep in class. Many have no bed of their own, sleeping with several other members of the family; some sleep on the floor.

Bed time is often a matter of choice rather than family regulation. A survey of 600 elementary students showed that over half regularly went to bed at 10:00 P.M. or later.

In low-income families there is little enough to provide the barest in food, shelter and clothes. A visit to the doctor or dentist is dictated only by pain or extreme need. In most deprived areas clinics provide some medical care, but there is little provision for dental care. The extent of dental needs in disadvantaged children is almost unbelievable. The writer was present when a dentist was examining a group of fifth and sixth graders and estimating the cost of dental repair for each. (Cost estimates were needed for establishing a dental program.) As he looked at each child, amounts like $100 and $150 were common. He saw no way of repairing one sixth grade boy's teeth short of pulling them and providing dentures.

Evaluating the School's Health Program

Surveys are only the first step in developing an effective health program. Health must be considered a primary objective of education in the disadvantaged school and in light of this, many steps follow the first.

---

[1] Frederick Robert Wilson, "Research Report on Family Health" (Monroe, Michigan). (Mimeographed)

The realistic principal accepts the fact that low-income parents cannot provide adequate health services. His efforts will be directed toward developing with teachers a program that will promote health care, protection and improvement, and working with the health department, social services, and service organizations to provide needed medical care for his students.

Developing an In-Service Health Program

Early in the school year an in-service education program in health should be held for all teachers. If it has not already been formed, this is the time to establish a health committee. Ideally, the committee will be composed of principal, classroom teachers, a physical education teacher, the school health nurse, a custodian, a lunchroom manager, a dentist, a doctor, a representative from a social service agency, one or more students and one or more parents.[2] Realistically, such a representation may not be possible, and dentist, doctor, social service personnel and parents may be asked to serve in an advisory role.

A chairman or coordinator of health services is needed in every school. If there is a full-time health nurse, this can fall within her scope of duties. Otherwise, the principal should assume this role since there are demands and meetings that make it difficult for a classroom teacher to meet.

An in-service program should include a review and discussion of school health policies. Such topics as first aid procedures, provisions for student illness, ways of reporting suspected communicable diseases, and other procedures should be clearly understood by all teachers.

School health services and their purposes should be on the agenda. The importance of vision and hearing screening tests should be stressed. Quite often school tests are the first to uncover hearing and sight impairments. In some cases when a child has a defect the school has not been informed by the parent and the disability has gone uncorrected.

The value of school health records needs to be emphasized. Teacher observations should be encouraged in detecting physical impairments that affect learning or need medical attention. There are some children who have learned to compensate for some deficiency, yet are not able to operate at peak performance. One especially observant fourth grade teacher discovered five sight problems in her room that had escaped previous attention. Study of past records showed a high transiency rate that had caused the children to miss every vision screening test to that time.

[2] The Michigan Department of Public Instruction, Bulletin No. 1030, *Self-Appraisal of the Health Program in Michigan Schools*, pp. 3-4.

Gearing the health program to community needs will produce an articulated program that includes: safety instruction, a clean environment, personal hygiene, the importance of proper rest, good nutrition, proper food preparation, causes and prevention of communicable diseases, the importance of regular medical and dental care, the importance of adequate immunizations, the harmful effects of smoking, drinking and drugs, and sex instruction.[3]

PROVIDING HEALTH INSTRUCTION

Safety Instruction

In areas where hopping between the cars of a slowly moving train or standing on the tracks of an oncoming train is considered an act of daring and courage, safety and the consequence of carelessness must be taught often.

The typical deprived youngster has far more than his share of hurts and accidents. This can be attributed, in part, to an environment that is conducive to hurts. Broken bottles, rusty nails, rotting boards, and other forms of refuse lend themselves to cuts, bruises, and breaks.

Another reason for the many accidents is the child himself. Left to his own devices he seems to have little fear of consequences of a dangerous act. One fourth grade child, who landed in a hospital unconscious for the better part of a day, after attempting to jump from playground "monkey bars" to a building window ledge, admitted he never gave a thought to the consequences if he missed.

Parents of the deprived talk much less to their offspring than do middle-class parents. Perhaps there are fewer warnings and cautions on their part for acts of danger and carelessness. In any event, the concerned disadvantaged school staff will keep the child aware of good safety practices.

Encouraging a Clean Environment

Cans, bottles, paper, and other forms of refuse are an accepted part of the disadvantaged youngster's world. Unless the school stresses pride in appearance, there is little likelihood that it will occur to any degree. In the elementary school this pride can be developed. Poster contests are effective ways to create interest and motivation. Establishing a playground pick-up for different classes is a practical, "doing" experience the

[3]*Ibid*, p. 9.

disadvantaged child likes. Awarding room pennants on a weekly basis for the cleanest room or the cleanest hall adds competition and constant awareness.

In the early grades, teachers who daily advocate "everything in its place, and a place for everything" are hoping for transfer of the habit to the home environment.

The year's culmination of a clean environment can be a "Clean-up, paint-up, fix-up" week. Such an undertaking can be handled better by some organization such as the Chamber of Commerce; however, it is not too large a project for a community school. Students who have been taught the value of picking up instead of dropping insure the success of such a project. The writer well remembers asking for 35 volunteers to give up a Saturday morning and clean up a park. Saturday he was met by 139 youngsters, enthusiastic and eager to work.

Personal Hygiene

Keeping clean can be a major task where no indoor plumbing facilities exist, crowded conditions make privacy a problem, and lack of clothes prevent frequent change. In light of these very real problems, instruction may center around how to take sponge baths, and how to wash out clothes by hand.

If facilities exist, the principal will find a shower program is well worth the time spent on it.

There are numerous sources of good, used clothing. Some women's clubs and organizations will contribute clothes. Managers of large chain stores are contacts that should not be overlooked. Quite often, through good will advertising, they will contribute discontinued items and clothes that have been returned due to flaws.

A parent organization is a prime source of used clothing. A community-wide clothing drive will turn up hundreds of usable items. The organization can then form committees for washing, mending, sizing, storing, and fitting when clothing is issued.

No matter how desperate the need, it is wise public relations to ask the parents' permission first. This can be done through a note or telephone call. Acceptance is usually quick and grateful. In the few cases where rejection occurs, stung pride usually asserts itself in new clothes for the child in question.

Certainly, in the light of resources available, no child should come to school smelling of urine because, as one child explained to her teacher, "I have to sleep with my baby sister who wets every night, and I don't have anything else to change to."

Proper Food Preparation

When surveys indicate that a majority of the student body is preparing one or more meals a day, school instruction should be provided.

After-school classes are best for instruction in food preparation. The class may be conducted by school personnel, although this is an excellent opportunity to call on community volunteers.

Boys will participate in greater numbers when they are separated from girls. Labeling their classes Junior Chefs, or some such title, gives a distinction that pleases and retains them. A well-planned, once-weekly, twelve or fourteen week course can provide solid, basic cooking instruction.

A culminating graduation effort has been effective in the writer's school in keeping up attendance. These efforts may include a smorgasbord to which the school staff, the students' parents, or both are invited to feast on their culinary productions.

Proper food preparation is a help but lack of adequate food remains a major problem in most deprived homes. Many disadvantaged schools offer a breakfast program for students. While cereal, milk, and juices are common fare, it can be as elaborate as funds and facilities permit. Such programs can be aided by federal funds.

Another common practice to alleviate poor nutrition is the milk and cookie mid-morning break for all students, kindergarten through sixth grade.

Medical and Dental Care

In most cases the disadvantaged child has an inordinate fear of a doctor or dentist. This is understandable, since only extreme pain or need receives medical attention. Typical of this fear is the boy who came to my office day after day with a toothache. When I finally secured funds to have his teeth cared for, he refused to go, stating: "I'd rather let them hurt and rot out than go to a dentist."

Arranging for visits of dentists and doctors to early elementary classrooms can help overcome this fear.

The school which is fortunate enough to share in government Title I ESEA funds should make money provisions for medical and dental services for children of the indigent. In addition to government grants, there are other resources to be tapped.

Check yourself. Do you know all the service organizations serving your school community? Who's the president of Rotary, Lions, Sertoma,

Kiwanis, The Optimists, and Exchange Club? What are their projects for the year? Can you persuade the Exchange Club to provide glasses for needy students? Will Rotary or Kiwanis purchase hearing aids? Will Sertoma provide funds to hire a dentist for a Summer Dental Program? The principal who is on a first name basis with service organization leaders and members will often be amazed at the quick response his requests elicit.

Religious Sponsoring Agencies are also sources of help and usually provide services on a non-sectarian basis.

Sex Instruction

Sex education classes may lead to some parent protest, although there is far less likelihood that wholesale objections that sometimes occur in middle-class communities will be encountered. Discussion of the program and its goals at parent meetings can help gain acceptance. Displays of materials used, with teachers available to explain content, and parent viewing of films used in instruction can help also in allaying parent qualms.

There is no doubt that sex instruction is needed early in the disadvantaged school. The deprived child meets sex in its rawest form. He learns of it in over-crowded home conditions, he encounters it as it is not-so-surreptitiously practiced in alleys and parked automobiles, and sex is more often than not *the* subject among his friends and acquaintances. With this experience, it is not surprising that he tries sex at an early age.

With this knowledge in mind, the concerned principal cannot delay sex instruction. The best program appears to be one that starts at kindergarten and is mandatory for all.

A complete program does not stop at reproduction but covers all aspects of sex instruction. Starting as early as grade five, emphasis should be placed on the ever-present danger of venereal disease. The positive benefits of not giving in to the easy philosophy of early sexual experimentation should be stressed. Forearmed with adequate knowledge, youngsters in their preteens, especially girls, have some realistic reasons with which to resist the advances of older boys who regard them as fair game for their pleasure.

Short of this extensive approach can be a program that depends upon parent approval and begins in the upper elementary grades. While less effective, it at least exposes children to some of the physical, emotional, psychological and social ramifications of sex.

Providing Health Services

A full-time or even part-time school nurse can be one of life's blessings for the overworked principal. Besides conducting yearly vision and hearing screening tests, she can be of great value in serving as a consultant to teachers in various aspects of the health program, in making home visits to parents, and in detecting handicaps and sicknesses of children.

An established need for a nurse's services can bring funding through Title I of the ESEA or support by a Community Action Program

Providing Health Education for Parents

There are many health factors and hazards in the home which the child can do little to control. The food he eats is the food his family provides. Home filth that breeds disease is more the responsibility of his parents, as is lack of immunizations against contagious disease. While the school can teach about the evils of smoking, drinking, and drugs, it will be of little worth unless the parents have the same concerns.

Parent-school organizations offer an excellent forum for instructing parents in sound health practices. For example, a film of a cancerous lung being removed is an impressive and long-remembered lesson on the effects of tobacco. Likewise, a film depicting the last stages of alcoholism or drug addiction is just as forceful and lasting in impression.

Evening classes for mothers in child and home care, cooking, and other areas of homemaking may improve conditions in some homes.

Of course, as every experienced principal knows, getting low-income parents to attend school programs is far from easy. Since, despite all blandishments, some parents refuse to attend any school function, home visits by a school nurse should be fully utilized if one is available.

And finally, of course, every principal in a deprived area has to accept the fact that he can't win 'em all. There are times when he must admit, "I failed." But the sting should be brushed away if he can say in the next breath, "But I tried."

CONSIDERING STUDENT ATTITUDES

Just as the home environment and health conditions affect the learning of the child, no less important is the child's outlook —the way he feels about the school, the people who work in it and most important of all—himself.

The child's attitude toward school will be, in part, a reflection of his parents'. The principal and his staff cannot operate from the premise that most parents and children understand the importance of an education. While it would seem logical to assume that, in general, disadvantaged students would regard school and teachers negatively, the extent of this negativism can be established by a simple survey.

Using the results of the survey, a concerned principal and his staff can find many ways to combat negative attitudes. The most obvious step is to make certain that the curriculum is geared to the abilities, interests and needs of the children. Success in school work is a powerful antidote to negativism. A staff-wide concentrated effort to make the children feel, "this is my school, I belong, and what I think is important," can change attitudes. For an example, children may be given the opportunity to help select books for the school library. The selection process has many educational implications, plus the built-in bonus that books the pupils select will receive more reading and better care. By the same token, children can be involved in the selection of *their* playground equipment. There are many other areas of school operation in which pupils can play a part.

An example of the effectiveness of student involvement is borne out by this incident. The writer knows of one school which planted shrubbery on two occasions, only to have it ripped out and destroyed. On the third occasion, the children were allowed to help make the selections and plant them. All but two plants survived, and those died of natural causes.

An effective administrative tack is to develop every possible idea that will create pupil pride in their school. Assembly programs featuring student talent, establishing a good athletic program, involving pupils as helpers in school activities, giving children many opportunities to perform for parents, displaying students' best work for public inspection, devoting one large bulletin board for pupil recognition, and planning special occasions such as school picnics at the beginning and end of the year are some ways of developing a feeling of, "This is my school and I'm glad I belong."

The importance of self-esteem in learning has been touched upon in an earlier chapter and will be developed more fully in chapters that follow. It bears repeating to point out that all teachers must be made aware of the importance of self-image in learning. A school survey of how pupils see themselves is worth devising and administering if it does nothing more than draw the staff's attention to this vital factor of learning.

The heartening fact about self-esteem is that it can be raised through principal and teacher concern and action. One teacher on the writer's staff who has remarkable success in working with children describes her method in this manner: "Every day I look for some way to make anyone who feels like a nobody feel like a somebody."

ESTABLISHING PRIORITIES THROUGH THE FACULTY SURVEY

Nobody knows more about the educational needs of deprived children than the understanding, concerned, experienced teachers who work with them day in and day out. Through the years they have learned the pitfalls to avoid and the paths to take. When it comes to establishing priorities, they know the wheat from the chaff. The principal who builds an effective program uses the knowledge and strength of his staff as the solid foundation.

If the principal has established an effective curriculum evaluation committee as described in Chapter 2, he will probably find the faculty survey superfluous. However, for a principal new to the job or new to the school, a survey can reveal essential information for starting out right with effective action.

An effective survey will consider all aspects of school operation and will be devised by principals and teacher representatives. By necessity it will be extensive, and adequate time should be given for its completion. The survey should be designed to establish immediate and long-range priorities.

In addition to in-service training, other major concerns would cover: pupil personnel educational services, curriculum revision and development, cultural enrichment programs, instructional materials, instructional equipment, professional reference materials, instructional organization, parent-community programs, school facilities and clerical services.

The results of the surveys indicate *what* is thought most important; the group and staff discussions that follow decide and plan *how* priorities will be met. Some identified needs require administrative action only, but the great majority will require cooperative effort of the staff and principal on a long-range basis. As an example, the problem of school drop-outs will rank high on elementary teachers' list of concerns. They see the drop-out syndrome begin early. Unless the child is "reached" and the spark ignited, teachers in the fourth and fifth grades can predict with all too much accuracy who will leave early and who will make it through.

A staff discussion on drop-outs might result in these suggested avenues of action.

1. Offer personal counseling.
2. Constantly stress the value of education — to parents as well as students.
3. Work with Big Brother and Big Sister Organizations.
4. Encourage parents to visit schools more often and show interest in students' work.
5. Use local businessmen as resource people.
6. Develop grade level units on the world of work and its requirements.
7. Fit curriculum to needs of children
8. Use more parent contacts and fewer report cards.
9. Place great importance on school attendance.
10. Work closely with Juvenile Court on chronic truancy problems.
11. Use drop-outs who later re-entered school as resource people.
12. Use former students who continued education as resource people.
13. Offer after-school, evening, and summer programs that change and improve student attitudes.
14. Provide personal tutoring for those experiencing significant learning problems.

When all the talking is done, it then becomes a matter of how to organize to get desired action.

If the reader has concluded that the results of a staff survey involve a great deal of work, his conclusions are correct. Nobody who knows has ever said administering or teaching in a disadvantaged school is easy. But the sweat is worth shedding and the challenges worth facing if only partial success is realized. In the game of educating disadvantaged kids, you use every trick you can to win. And in this game it matters greatly whether you win or lose.

SUMMARY

The deprived child comes to school with a multitude of deficits. However, he is basically like all other children in that he needs acceptance and understanding. The basic needs of food, clothes and emotional well-being must first be considered in educating the disadvantaged.

Principals should not assume that every child fits the "typical" disadvantaged mold. There are degrees of deprivation. The poor of suburban communities are generally less deprived than children from the large cities.

Home environment factors play an important part in the child's learning. Surveys of home conditions can establish parent support of school and other important information. Information supplied by surveys should result in corresponding action. Easy answers are not found and should not be expected.

The school's health program should undergo regular and systematic evaluation. A health committee should be formed to promote and coordinate health services. A well-rounded health program strives to encourage the student to be aware of and practice good safety and health habits. Physical needs of clothing and food can be provided through help of organizations and government funding. Frequently service organizations can be persuaded to provide money for medical and dental care. The school health program should extend to the parents, since home inadequacies and practices are responsible for unhealthful conditions.

Pupil attitudes toward themselves, the school, and teachers are determinants in the amount of learning that takes place.

A faculty survey will indicate those areas the staff feels should receive immediate attention. Planning and follow-up should occur as soon as it is feasible.

5

Instructing Deprived Children

In the press of all the school business clamoring for attention, the principal of the disadvantaged school may be tempted to shunt aside curriculum matters. He cannot submit to this temptation for his role as an instructional leader should rank at the very top of his job responsibilities.

A planned portion of every day should be spent with teachers in establishing the proper climate for optimum learning, in deciding with his staff what should be taught, and providing materials and means, to the best of his ability, to instruct pupils in the most meaningful manner.

An effective principal keeps in close contact with the classrooms. In this manner he stays fully aware of student problems and the problems that they, in turn, create for the teachers.

If it can be justly said by classroom teachers: "He doesn't know what is going on in the classroom," it should be added: "He doesn't deserve the mantle of leadership."

Teaching deprived kids is a big job and it is too much to meet all the needs a classroom of students contains. The principal must become a supporter of teacher efforts and make as many moves as a master chess player to supply special help the teacher must have to be effective.

DEVELOPING THE LEARNING CLIMATE

If the principal has laid his groundwork well, he has a good knowledge of his staff's strengths and weaknesses. An "open door" policy and close working relationship assure this. Even with new teachers, if the orientation process has been thorough, as outlined in Chapter 1, there is much essential information he already has at hand.

The constant theme of "know your students, learn their backgrounds" should almost become a Phillipic. This effort is made with the purpose and hope that teacher insights will deepen and classroom performance will improve. However, full awareness of all the environmental conditions in a slum community can be so large as to overwhelm many teachers. To avert resignation or hopelessness the principal and staff should realistically develop a working philosophy of what can be changed, what can be accepted, and what is beyond the power of the school.

Working for Good Pupil-Teacher Relations

Pupil-teacher clashes are frequent in slum schools, and not every clash is the pupil's fault. The teacher with a serious flaw in attitude, methods, or organization is headed for serious trouble in the disadvantaged school. These children, environmentally conditioned, are experts at testing and probing and quick to exploit a weakness. The principal should not hesitate to step in and counsel a teacher when he sees any personal characteristic or approach that is unsuccessful. At stake are the children's education and a teacher's career. As the school leader he cannot afford to overlook either.

The importance of mutual liking between students and teacher has been touched upon in another chapter. It has been the observation of the writer that teachers with a "firm accepting" philosophy have been the most successful in establishing rapport. Illustrative of this is a fourth grade teacher's comment: "I know what I will hear and not hear, what I will see and not see, and then I set a few clearly understood rules and enforce them"

Another well-liked and respected sixth grade teacher was in agreement when he said:

> Every day I try to get the message across, "Look, I'm your friend. I understand your problems and why you act the way you do. But there are limits beyond which you can't go and if you do something is going to happen every time."

A poll of upper elementary disadvantaged students, asking: "What do you consider a good teacher?" revealed the following characteristics that differ little from those advanced by middle-class children.

1. They should like their students.
2. They should be fair.
3. They should be fun.

4. They should be interesting to listen to.

5. They should help students.

Such a survey substantiates a veteran teacher's observation: "The children can be reached. It just takes more imagination, more work, and more time."

The accepting teacher listens, encourages, assists and shows concern for his student's progress and welfare. In an accepting climate the student learns that his opinions do count.

Student Deficits and Strengths

The educational plight of deprived children is well-known by almost everyone in academic circles. The lack of verbal ability, motivation and curiosity, poor self-image and all the other gaps must speak volumes to the principal and his staff.

The mounting evidence that slum children fall farther behind each year in school mandates that educational cancer must be attacked early with every means possible. A remedial reading teacher of many years' experience substantiated this viewpoint when she said, "If we don't catch these children up in reading skills and vocabulary by the end of the third grade, I'm convinced we've pretty much lost the battle."

Realistic instruction, of course, is based on the needs of the children and every staff member must be fully aware of these needs. However, it is important to know why these deficits exist, and, just as important, to identify the strengths of the underprivileged.

It is easy to overlook the fact that deprived children have potential. Their limited vocabulary is due to the low educational attainment of community inhabitants, lack of opportunity to speak with elders, and lack of reading materials and travel experiences, to name a few. It cannot be forgotten that verbal skills can be acquired. Abraham Lincoln emerged from a deprived background to command the English language as few Americans ever learned to do.

Lack of motivation is a constant obstacle to getting through to disadvantaged children. They, and often their parents, see little relevance in education. But equally often, lack of motivation is caused by a teacher who is trying to present material the student neither wants to know nor understands. Evidence of this is the fact that every slum school has its miserable failures while down the hall other teachers are successful in reaching their pupils.

The fact that deprived children have acquired skills should not be overlooked. While it is true that most are not school oriented skills, they have been learned to meet specific needs.

The adaptability of deprived youngsters is full evidence of their learning ability. Left more on their own to fend for themselves, they learn early to furnish their own amusement, cook their own meals, dress themselves and cope with a constantly challenging neighborhood environment. These and other student strengths are excellent building blocks for a need-fulfilling program.

Asking Essential Educational Questions

Socrates, that persistent questioner, set the model for all who would administer or teach in a disadvantaged school. The questioning habit requires answers and reasons for decisions and prevents hasty, make-shift programs.

In the disadvantaged school, one must constantly ask: "How much is this child ready to learn?" The answer comes only after thorough background study and realistic evaluation.

Equally important is: How much does this child need to know? Other questions flow from this in rapid order. What is his potential? Will the education provided him meet practical needs? Equip him for possible future alternatives?

What shall this child be taught? Reading and math only? What of his moral values? Can we afford to ignore lying, stealing, cheating, contempt of laws, irresponsibility?

What organization shall we use? The graded, textbook oriented approach? Nongraded? Pupil-tailored individualized instruction?

These and other questions that have no easy answers must be asked. There are general answers for deprived children but no pat answers for a deprived child. But the fact that these questions involve searching thought is all the more reason why they should be asked.

PROVIDING MATERIALS AND EQUIPMENT FOR INSTRUCTION

The pupil-tailored program loses its effectiveness unless proper, adequate materials are supplied. To achieve this, the principal must sometimes become a procurer, diplomat and persuader.

Inappropriate instructional materials are an educational obstacle that most every disadvantaged school staff must face. In many school districts, finances is the bugaboo. Unfortunately, in the deprived districts where the need is greatest, indifference and apathy of the voters is also the highest.

The principal must learn the power of advertising. If it sells foot powder, why not education? Every principal should map a plan of action that lets people in on what is happening at his school. This is time well-spent, for a "No" vote on a school millage issue can effectively tie the hands of a school staff striving for a sound educational program.

Probably more often than lack of finances, inappropriate materials emerge from a district-wide textbook selection policy. This time-honored procedure assumes that every child is alike and a textbook will supply most of his educational needs. It is not easy to break this chain of thinking, for there are financial and procedural benefits the district gains from mass purchases. The principal and his staff in the low-income community must have adequate proof at hand that the student body is different, have the courage to say it (low-income parents often resent hearing their children have greater needs than middle-class children), and the persistence to keep working for materials suited to the student body.

Selection of Materials and Equipment

The effective staff evaluation committee, discussed in Chapter 2, keeps an up-to-date, general evaluation of materials and equipment of instruction. Areas of strengths, weaknesses and recommendations are readily available for staff use.

To facilitate efficient operation, a materials selection committee can be formed. The principal and a teacher representative from each grade level constitutes a workable group. It is incumbent upon the committee to keep the whole staff abreast of its proceedings, to solicit teacher opinions and suggestions, and to get final approval from the staff before materials are purchased. Funds, the special needs of the pupils, and the learning value of materials will determine the selections.

If a school is fortunate enough to have Title I ESEA funds available, most essential equipment to meet educational goals can be acquired. Without these funds, strict priorities will need to be established and observed.

Books on a high interest, low difficulty level, designed to encourage independent reading, are needed in abundance. As one student succinctly stated: "You ain't learnin' if you ain't readin', and you ain't readin' if you don't understand what you're readin'."

The child of the deprived lives in a concrete world. Abstractions frustrate and turn him off. His sensory-poor training leaves him without refined discrimination in the areas of sight, sound and touch. Lack of verbal skills loom as ever larger handicaps as he grows older and expands his contacts.

These skills can be developed through audiovisual materials and their proper use. Charts, pictures, filmstrips, films, kits, overhead projector transparencies, globes, tape recorders, records, etc., should be regarded as basic learning tools.

Inherent in the use of audiovisual equipment is educational, purposeful planning. If their use is not related to classroom needs, the films and records merely become a pleasant, meaningless interlude. The deprived child is too far behind to afford such classroom luxuries.

Any number of guidelines have been developed to implement the use of audiovisual aids. These can usually be obtained free of charge from supply companies and adapted to specific school needs. The wise principal will not expend thousands of dollars in materials and equipment without taking this last step to insure that their use strengthens the educational efforts of his staff.

PROVIDING SPECIAL HELP

The disadvantaged school is faced with problems of providing direct service to children who are emotionally disturbed, mentally retarded, physically handicapped, school alienated, and physically abused. To meet this task a full range of special services personnel is needed. An adequate program should include:

- Psychological testing of children in need of help.
- Classes for the mentally retarded, both educable and trainable.
- Special classes for disturbed children.
- Guidance counselor to assist children from regular classrooms.
- School social workers to help children and parents.
- Psychiatric consultation on a periodic basis.
- Speech therapy.
- Orthopedic classrooms.
- Homebound program for extended student illnesses.
- Classes for partially-sighted and deaf.

Some of these programs may serve more than one school, for example, deaf and partially sighted. Of course, it is beyond the power of the building principal to provide these programs unless personnel, facilities, and funds are made available. When they are lacking he must be fully aware that special mental and physical problems can rarely be met in the regular classroom, and that children left to vegetate in a failure-doomed situation usually become a disturbing factor to the teacher and other pupils. It then becomes his duty to point this out to the powers-that-be and indicate a willingness to do anything necessary to help provide the needed services.

The Role of Special Services Personnel

It is unwise for a principal to assume that all his classroom teachers know the role of the specialists who serve his building. This is borne out by the wry comment of a school social worker: "I've served this building three years and 25 percent of the kids referred to me are completely inappropriate."

As coordinator of his building's program, the principal simply can't allow the left hand to be unaware of what the right is doing. Much confusion can be eliminated by giving special service personnel time during staff meetings to explain their roles and responsibilities. Of course, such understanding is a two way street, and the principal must be aware of those specialists without classroom teaching experience and make certain that they understand the functions and responsibilities of this invaluable general practitioner of education.

An assessment sheet, such as that which follows, is an excellent means of arriving at special problems. A number of these should be distributed to teachers early in the school year. After they have been completed, the problems are categorized and the principal, specialist or specialists concerned, and the classroom teacher discuss the problem. Out of this discussion emerges the best prescriptive decision possible.

ASSESSMENT OF PROBLEMS

Name _____ Grade _____
Teacher _____

Assessment of Problems:
1. What is your assessment of his potential for success in your classroom? (Record as a grade, A, B, C, D, E)
2. Does he or she have poor study habits? (Record as good, inconsistent, poor, other, explain why not known)
3. Does he or she have poor peer relations? (Record as good, inadequate, negative influence on desirable school behavior, other, explain)
4. Pupil-Teacher Relations
   a. Is he or she able to ask for help from the teacher? (Record as often, seldom, never, other, explain)

b. Is he or she disrespectful toward the teacher? (Record as often, seldom, never, other, explain)

5. This student will, in my opinion . . .

    _____ a.   Have serious difficulty getting through school.

    _____ b.   Have considerable difficulty getting through school.

    _____ c.   Have some difficulty getting through school.

    _____ d.   Have little difficulty getting through school.

    _____ e.   Have no difficulty getting through school.

    _____ f.   Other (explain)

6. Which of the following suggestions do you feel would assist this pupil? (Please ask the teacher to use priorities—1,2,3)

    _____ a.   Individual tutorial service

    _____ b.   Curriculum change . . .

        _____ 1.   Into ungraded program

        _____ 2.   Enrichment of present program, with field trips, better materials, or individual attention through teacher helpers

        _____ 3.   Present situation okay if teacher can find places to isolate pupil within classroom when his or her behavior is disrupting the classroom process

        _____ 4.   Placement outside the classroom with children with similar problems (children who are slow learners, socially maladjusted or emotionally disturbed)

        _____ 5.   Into a Special Education program

    _____ c.   Individual Services (counseling or social work)

    _____ d.   Group Service (group counseling or social group work)

    _____ e.   Remedial reading help

    _____ f.   Remedial arithmetic help

    _____ g.   Services to family

    _____ h.   Consultation with you about classroom handling techniques

    _____ i.   Special teacher to help with perceptual difficulties

    _____ j.   Crisis teacher or helping teacher part-time or temporary

An example of the kind of program that can result from cooperative principal-specialist-classroom teacher action is the Social Group Work Program conducted in the writer's school by the school social worker.

Later elementary pupils, identified by their teachers as needing help in social or academic skills, are grouped carefully so that each child will be helped by the group experience and also have something to offer to the group. For example, Johnny may be withdrawn, but a whiz at basketball. He can be helped by Joe, who has poor coordination, and yet be helped by Ted who is outgoing and socially accepted.

Teachers keep the groups flexible so that if a child improves sufficiently, he can be moved out and replaced by another child who needs help. The emphasis is on a positive approach to problem solving, self-determination, and assuming responsibility for one's own behavior.

Out of this program conducted by the same dedicated person grew a group of mothers who meet in various homes and discuss their children's school problems and school adjustment.

APPROACHES AND TEACHING IDEAS THAT WORK

It is a fruitless exercise to try to cram unwanted knowledge into deprived pupils. One is never left to guess about the success or failure of a teacher to reach disadvantaged children. Failure results in overt manifestations of lack of attention, whispering, moving about the room, general restlessness and incomplete work.

The most successful teachers are those who involve pupils in the learning process. When children are given a voice in their learning, it becomes readily apparent that they favor "doing" exercises such as experiments and class projects; activities that offer competition and reachable goals; learning situations outside the textbook such as audiovisual materials, field trips and assemblies; and classroom instruction that grows out of their own interests, conditions and desires.

It is a normal reaction for students with reading problems to shy away from activities centered around a textbook. Whether the pupil increases or decreases his textbook dislike depends upon the teacher. Staff members who hit for a high average use the book as a home base and spread out from that point.

Making Reading Come Alive

Dramatization is a love and strength of deprived children. They delight in play acting at all ages. Any reading text worth adopting in a disadvantaged school should have several selections at every level written for and adaptable to dramatization. Puppets should be standard equipment in early elementary classes. Some teachers have found children furnishing voices for puppets who refused to talk otherwise. Puppet shows, based on textbook stories, can inspire interest in reading.

Plays in upper elementary classes bring similar success. "Hansel and Gretel" and similar stories, performed in class, read into a tape recorder or performed on a stage, can teach more about inflection and expression than a year of lectures on inattentive ears.

Building sets, painting scenery, staging, and acting a play, as one successful sixth grade teacher observed, "is an object lesson to everyone that words can tell you what to do, show you how to do it, yet allow you to use them in the way that is best for you." Thus when Sally learns she excels as a witch but Harry is better as some other character, the first glimmer of the power of words begins to break through.

The basic needs of all human beings are the same and the heady thrill of applause for a performance can give a boost to low self-esteem and create the desire to repeat the success.

Interest Arousing Approaches

Many educators have cautioned against competition in elementary education, warning of the harm that may result from tension and failure. The deprived child lives in a competitive world and he will respond to goals that are *realistic* and *reachable.*

Spelling baseball is used effectively with lower elementary children. Race, a similar game in which children's names are placed at a starting gate and moved across the chalk board with successful answers, can be used in almost any subject area. Word games similar to Bingo or popular card games are effective motivators.

Travel brochures can provide learning in many areas. Planning a vacation requires reading for accommodations, rates, places of interest, routes to be followed, miles to be traveled, suitable clothing to be taken, and all the other matters that must be considered.

Many teachers still harbor the idea that learning isn't taking place when children are having fun. The day of the fire and brimstone preacher has long passed and it is high time this Puritan thinking be banished from education.

A mail order catalogue is an effective teaching aid. When an upper elementary teacher hands out catalogs and announces: "You have $87 to spend. You can purchase three items and they must come to a total of between $86 and $87," he has given an exercise in practical living which the children understand.

A "Dine Out" is an effective way to teach etiquette and manners. Children are motivated to learn because the culmination is dining out in a restaurant. Service organizations can be persuaded to provide the money.

Most teachers would never dare to assign a theme or original story. And yet it can be achieved if children are allowed to choose their own topics, allowed natural use of language and are assured grading will not be used. A class vote may also decide not to use names.

A sixth grade teacher, who has used this approach with great success, has received stories that range from one boy's revelation that he intended to kill himself because of home conditions to a girl's delightful fantasy of an "off and on rainbow."

Another teacher, with a knack for getting the most from deprived pupils, states: "Once you get them started, don't hurry them. If you do, they feel you don't trust them to do it on their own. When you get the majority of the group with you, the rest will usually try so they don't stand out as different."

Individual Pupil Work Plans

Just as involvement of the teachers in curriculum is the key to workable programs, so is involvement of the students in their class work. When students are given the opportunity to develop their own work plans (with teacher help of course), evaluate their own efforts, and state their ideas of what they would like to do, it is hard for them to pass off the work as "teacher stuff."

A work plan not only works, but it is one step toward individualized instruction, the approach that appears to hold the most promise in meeting disadvantaged pupils' needs.

Work plans are successful for the following reasons:

1. They allow the student to work on subject assignments in the order of his own preference.
2. They teach the value of planning, following a schedule, and wise use of time.
3. They provide the opportunity for the student to evaluate his own effort and learn the relation of grades to honest effort and achievement.
4. The student is given the opportunity to do extra work which results in special recognition.

The mechanics of the work plan can be as varied as the ideas of the pupils and teachers. The example here is one devised by a sixth grade class and teacher.

MY WORK PLANS FOR TODAY   Special Notes:
Name _____
Date _____

Special things today — *time?*   Science
    Spanish _____   Reading group _____
    Art _____   Program _____
    Music _____   Library _____
    Gym _____

Arithmetic — topic _____   Reading
Assignment _____
Make-up work_____
Extra Work _____

Social Studies: Topic_____   Health
Geography, History:
    Assignment _____
    Make-up Work _____
    Extra Work _____

Spelling — Writing   Things I would like to
                                              do — Projects

Language   Extra   books   I   am
                                              reading

Evaluation: How I   *Evaluation:* How I
think I did my work today (check one)   think I could improve:
A ___ B ___ C ___ D ___ E ___

Using Trips to Teach

A bus can be a rolling learning laboratory. The well-planned field trip that is an extension of classroom teaching has great educational value.

The principal and his staff should cooperatively develop guidelines that insure maximum benefits. Along with the guideline, suggested trips should be developed for each grade. This avoids duplication of the same trips for different grades, encourages planning, and leads to a variety of experiences. An example of a worthwhile field trip for older children is a court visit. Children of the slums have hostility for law enforcement officers and open contempt for courts. They have seen wrong-doers get by without punishment and have often been victims themselves of a theft, extortion, or beating.

Such a visit can arise from class discussions on the need for laws and the necessity for obeying them.

Pupils should be included in pre-planning. If money is involved, they should be allowed a voice in the decision of how much to take. When money is required, there is always the problem of those who do not have it. The principal should try to establish some fund to handle these exigencies and provide dignified ways for the students to earn it.

Parents should be notified of all field trips through a note or letter similar to the following. This not only serves as a means of keeping them aware of what is happening in school, but encourages home discussion of trip experiences.

Dear Parents:

In the interests of promoting good citizenship, our sixth grade children will observe a trial in Circuit Court. The judge explains Court procedure, and the children have the opportunity to see how a jury is picked, how witnesses are interviewed, and learn other necessary matters pertaining to a trial.

The trial is scheduled to begin at 9 A.M. There is always the possibility that the case will be settled out of court, but if so, the judge will take the group on a tour and explain the Court set-up and answer questions.

If parents wish to accompany the group, they are welcome to come with the class.

Field trips, class activities, dramatization, all succeed more often when pupils have a voice in their planning.

A principal does not play a passive role in teacher ideas and approaches used in the classroom. He helps keep the educational program strong by suggesting ideas, encouraging teachers to try their own, and assisting them in every possible way in their efforts. It may be that the principal plays his most important role by creating a flexible learning climate which allows and encourages his staff to meet the extraordinary needs of their charges in innovative, functional ways.

SUMMARY

The principal must regard his role as instructional leader the most important of his responsibilities. Development of curriculum should be a joint effort of principal and staff.

Some essential prerequisites to teaching deprived children are: student background information, mutual teacher-pupil liking, a firm accepting teacher attitude.

Student strengths are evidence of learning ability and are excellent starting points for a need-fulfilling program.

A materials and equipment selection committee, composed of principal and staff members, can purchase utilitarian books, machines, and materials when well thought out guidelines are followed.

As coordinator of his building's program, the principal makes his staff aware of the help available from special services personnel. A prepared problem assessment sheet, distributed to the teachers, is an excellent means of keeping the principal and special service personnel aware of special classroom problems.

Drama is a love and strength of disadvantaged students and can be used to arouse interest in reading.

Classroom activities that have a practical, concrete approach, and which involve pupils in planning and selection, have the best chance of succeeding with disadvantaged children.

6

Evaluating Students
in the Disadvantaged School

The principal must keep uppermost in mind the fact that the attitudes and reactions of disadvantaged children toward standardized tests are much different from those of middle-class children. The middle-class child's "do as well as I can" philosophy may be countered by the deprived's "guessing game," "mark any old thing" or quitting attitude. Teachers who have seen what tests do to their children and what their children do to tests have opinions that range from reservations to open contempt for all test results. Added to these is the near impossibility of finding "culture fair" tests which are couched in the language of the child and not the abstract, symbol laden language of the authors.

In the face of these obstacles, it is probably safe to say that every principal of a disadvantaged school has entertained grave doubts about the worth of a standardized testing program. Despite these doubts, he knows that some form of assessment is needed if for no other reason than to measure the effectiveness of the educational program in meeting the needs of the children.

ARRIVING AT A TESTING PHILOSOPHY

The beginning of every sound testing program starts with the deceptively appearing simple question: What are we testing for? It is erroneous to believe that every teacher has the answer to this question. Some, who have little faith in test results, may assume it is a time-wasting exercise demanded by the school administration.

85

Finding Teacher Opinions

A questionnaire survey[1] can help establish what the teachers feel are important in a group testing program. If teacher opinions are incorporated in the program there will be greater understanding of objectives and wider use of results.

A survey of one staff revealed how they viewed the purposes of group testing.

Finding areas of strength and weakness in a child	First Priority
Obtaining instructional level of a child	Second Priority
Screening for further diagnosis	Third Priority
Finding individual growth rates	Fourth Priority
Finding child's specific knowledge of facts	Fifth Priority
Comparing school with national norms	Sixth Priority

These findings indicated a real desire on the part of the teachers to establish where the child was operating academically in order that he might be instructed from that level.

The same questionnaire revealed that teachers of the disadvantaged felt grade equivalent scores on achievement tests were not accurate rankings and achievement tests did not provide accurate information. The degree of distrust ranged from:

"Standardized tests alone do not give a true picture of the children's abilities. They must be substantiated by informal assessments, observations and teacher made tests" to . . .

"Standardized tests are so unrealistic in our situation I rarely ever look at results anymore."

Parents Should Be Asked

Many principals are opposed to involving parents in the testing program. One acquaintance typified this attitude when he remarked:

"There's no use getting parents stirred up about tests and get them to meddling in something they know nothing about."

Involving parents means respecting their rights and opinions rather than expecting them to actually help make test selections. Every parent should have the basic right to know about instruments that measure his child's ability, achievement and problem areas.[2]

[1] Frederick Robert Wilson, "Group Testing Questionnaire Survey" (Monroe, Michigan), p. 2. (Mimeographed).

[2] *The Use and Misuse of Tests*, State Guidance Committee, Publication 516 (Lansing, Michigan, 1961), p. 6.

Results of a parent survey in one community revealed that most parents knew very little about the testing program and had little understanding of how to interpret the results of standardized achievement tests. This lack of understanding is probably typical of most deprived communities and points up the need for presenting more essential information on testing to parents. This can be done in a simple, non-technical manner in parent meetings and through interpretation of teachers at parent-teacher conferences.

Don't Forget to Ask the Children

The object of all the evaluation is rarely asked to state his opinions on the instruments used. It is assumed that he will be opposed to testing and that his lack of training and objectivity will lead to worthless conclusions.

There is no doubt that a survey of students in a disadvantaged school will reveal general opposition to tests. However, older elementary children are surprisingly perceptive in their evaluation of instruments and their criticisms are worthy of consideration.

The following statements are representative of comments made by upper elementary children when they were asked their opinions of standardized tests.

"The words are too long and I don't understand them"

"There's too much to do and I worry that I won't get done."

"There's too much reading and it's too hard. I think we get tests so the teachers will know how well we understand things."

When all opinions of those affected by the tests are known and considered, selection of tests that are realistic in light of the school population and more palatable to teachers and students should result. Wise initial test selection is just the beginning not the end. There must be provisions for continuous review, revisions when necessary, and an ongoing, in-service program on the use and interpretation of tests. This assures a testing program that will provide useful information about the educational progress of individual children, help indicate the effectiveness of the curriculum in meeting children's needs, and be used by the teachers to improve instruction.

A staff group testing committee is the most effective means of making certain these criteria are met.

PROVIDING AN EFFECTIVE GROUP TESTING COMMITTEE

Selection of Members

The testing committee will be no more effective than the people who comprise its membership. The principal, without appearing to "stack" the committee, should select those people who have the most knowledge of and most concern for the testing program.

In a large school the following members could provide valuable services to the committee.

Ex Officio Members
The Superintendent of Schools
The Assistant Superintendent for Instruction
The Curriculum Coordinator
The Director of Reading

Staff Membership
The Principal
The School Diagnostician
The Teacher Representative from Each Grade Level

Functions of the Testing Committee

The tasks of the testing committee are varied and comprehensive. This fact must be taken into account when setting up each meeting agenda, or there is a danger that too much will be attempted and nothing done well.

The normal business procedures will be a constant effort to balance the technical aspects of testing against the practical aspects of the school situation. For an example, after developing guidelines for test selection, some tests that meet most criteria will be discarded because scores are too heavily dependent on reading ability, a definite disadvantage to the disadvantaged.

In addition to establishing criteria for test selection, review of the existing program is needed every year. An analysis of test results may reveal that far too many children are scoring extremely low on a given achievement test and far too few scoring in the upper levels. What is wrong? Is it the test? The curriculum? Something wrong with the norms? Answers must be sought and found before continuing the program.

Perhaps a revision or change appears necessary. A careful analysis must be made before such a step is recommended. Discarding a long-used test is certain to bring howls of protest from some quarters. Despite these objections, if a change appears to be for the better, such a recommendation should be made.

The committee can never shake the specter of cost. There must be a constant comparison between cost and efficiency of the program. Such a study may reveal that there is too much testing in a system. Could the program be streamlined? Would four achievement tests prior to grade seven be as effective as one every year? Would three aptitude tests prior to grade seven be sufficient for teacher use? These and myriad other questions arise and require decisions throughout the year.

Interpreting the Program

A key function of the committee is interpretation to the staff and parents. Understanding the purpose of testing and how to interpret results are as important to unlocking meaningful information as the Rosetta Stone was to Egyptian hieroglyphics. The greatest abuse and misuse of tests falls in the area of misinterpretation.

Written communications can help keep the staff informed. Written minutes of each committee meeting should be kept for general dissemination.

A guidebook giving general information about testing, and instructions on interpreting and using specific tests administered in the school helps assure better utilization of measurements. Valuable as written communications may be, they should be considered only as supplements to staff meetings and in-service training sessions. As Cleopatra discovered early, there's nothing more effective than face-to-face communication.

The training sessions should be reasonably non-technical and aimed at showing the teachers how test results can help them in their business of teaching kids.

Audiovisual methods are especially effective. Tapes, records and films often do mean "more than a thousand" lecture words, although role-playing between teachers who are "test wise" can be stimulating and revealing.

At all times the testing committee should take careful pains to dispel the idea that they constitute the last word on testing. Suggestions and recommendations should be solicited from the staff.

Statements such as these, made by teachers at a meeting, can help in decision making.

"Tests should be scored by the classroom teacher, not machines. This enables her to obtain a clearer picture of her class as well as each child."

"In a disadvantaged school IQ tests should not be given below third grade. Tests below third are largely invalid and may damage a child if the teacher assumes an expectancy level that is not realistic."

Evaluation should not be restricted to students alone. If the testing committee provides a means for evaluating its own performance, it will help make each succeeding presentation more effective. A few easily answered questions can obtain the needed information.

GROUP TESTING EVALUATION[3]

Dear Teacher: We would like your help in insuring that we obtain the best possible results from our group testing program. Would you please answer the following questions about your experiences with this phase of our group testing program so that we may evaluate our efforts.

INSTRUCTIONS ON ADMINISTRATION

1. Did you receive instructional material on the administration of the tests you were to give?   YES ___ NO ___
2. Were the instructional materials you received sufficiently clear?   YES ___ NO ___
   IF NOT, in what ways were they confusing? _____
   _____
   _____
3. Did they leave you with any unanswered questions? YES ___ NO ___
   IF YOU HAD QUESTIONS THAT WERE NOT ANSWERED, what kinds of questions did you have?
   _____

TEST BOOKLETS AND ANSWER SHEETS

1. Did you have sufficient quantities of test booklets and answer sheets?   YES ___ NO ___
2. Did your class, as a whole, seem to be able to handle the test without undue frustration?   YES ___ NO ___
3. Did you have any particular problems in administration of the test, such as with time limits, filling out answer sheets, etc.?   YES ___ NO ___
   IF SO, what kinds of problems did you have? _____
   _____

PROBLEMS WITH INDIVIDUAL CHILDREN

Did you notice any children in your class having difficulties; e.g., throwing-up, giving-up, answering randomly, acting frightened, etc.?   YES ___ NO ___

[3] Karl D. Furr and Frederick Robert Wilson, "Group Testing Evaluation" (Monroe, Michigan). (Mimeographed)

If a teacher indicates problems with individual children, a report should be requested. The report can be the basis of counseling or retesting or both.

INDIVIDUAL PROBLEM REPORT

Dear Teacher: The scores children receive on a group test can be put to many uses. Some of these involve the creation of educational prescriptions for the individual child and the diagnosis of individual education problems. Since the worth of the judgments made about an individual child based on his group test scores rests very heavily on how meaningful that score is, we would like your help in identifying individual children who had problems with the test they just took. If any of the children in your class taking this test seemed extremely anxious, frightened, worried, or scared, if anyone seemed to give up or answer the questions by randomly marking answers, or if anyone got sick or in other ways indicated they could not handle the test, please indicate the child's name and the kind of problem he seemed to be having.

TEST_____GRADE_____DATE____

<u>NAME OF CHILD</u>   <u>PROBLEM HE SEEMED TO BE HAVING</u>

_____

_____

_____

If you have any additional comments you would like to make about the way the class as a whole reacted to the test, please indicate them below.

_____

_____

_____

RETURN TO: GROUP-TESTING COMMITTEE

TEACHER _____ SCHOOL _____

Prior to acceptance of the job, every member must be made aware that membership on the testing committee requires hours of extra time, study and service. His remuneration can come in the form of more valid test results that will, hopefully, bring student designed instruction.

IMPORTANT FACTORS IN ASSESSMENT OF DISADVANTAGED STUDENTS

If the writer's staff is typical, most teachers in disadvantaged schools see some value in standardized testing. However, all have reservations which they are quick to point out.

The background of the child is always a concern. What effect does lack of newspapers, magazines and books in the home have on school achievement? Is he penalized for lack of travel experience? For things he has never seen? Can he be expected to know horses graze in pastures if he doesn't know what a pasture is?

It cannot be assumed that every home in a deprived area lacks cultural advantages, and not every child in the area is denied travel experiences and books in the home. The best way of establishing the home conditions is to encourage parent contacts and home visitations. Short of this, a simple questionnaire can help determine the extent of cultural deprivation.

The feelings a child has about his school and teacher are important. If he considers school a place where good times can be had, a student's reaction to any kind of school work will be much different from one who considers school some sort of frustrating prison.

Teacher-student sessions can uncover attitudes and feelings if they are not openly apparent.

Anecdotal reports should be kept on students whose school work is affected by hostility toward school or teachers. This will help future teachers in making evaluations and adjustments.

When viewed on a large scale, a surprising number of disadvantaged children feel they are not liked by their teachers. When questioned why they feel this way, most frequently mentioned reasons are teacher scoldings and the fact that other students get to do more things than they.

The unfortunate fact that discipline plays such a major role in disadvantaged schools keeps the teacher stern and firm far more than he would prefer.

The typical deprived child has learned far less how to share than his middle-class peers. In an environment where it is often a fight to get and keep what he wants, it is easy to think of self first and feel the other person is getting the breaks.

Disadvantaged youngsters are no different from other students in that they work better for a teacher they like and one they feel likes them. Teachers must take student feelings toward them in account and find ways of showing their friendly human side as well as their firm, fair teacher image. The most successful teachers are those who can let down outside the classroom. Joining games on the playground and planning extra-curricular affairs can persuade most that the teacher is "a pretty nice person who likes us kids."

Countless reams have been written about the importance of self-concept in learning. In dealing with the deprived, no other factor assumes more importance. Unless he feels good about himself there is no motivation to try, no perceived need to attend school regularly, no effort to conform to school rules—all steps down the stairway of school failure and dropping out at the first opportunity.

The child of the streets is far less likely to come to school with a positive self-image. Younger elementary children are usually the butt of the frustrations and agressions of the older and bigger. Their lack of confidence and unworthiness often causes them to think that school is too hard and the teacher unfair in asking them to do more than they can.

Such an attitude can play havoc with standardized tests. Looking at a test using words unfamiliar to them, on a plane above their reading level, and asking them to black out dots on an answer sheet are more than many students are willing to tackle. "Then," according to a veteran teacher, "they begin the 'guessing game,' the 'let's see who can finish quickest game.' or 'to heck with this stuff, I quit' attitude."

The effective teacher in the disadvantaged school spends hours on motivation and ideas that produce success. He plans praises, prods and primes until every child in his class gets the feeling he can do the work. Only then can he be as assured as the teacher who told his reluctant sixth grader, "Let's not try to fool ourselves that you can't do this work, Joe. Let's just be honest and say you don't feel like working today."

Some children simply can't work in large groups. For them individual testing will be necessary. Individual tests in various curriculum areas can be invaluable in establishing a child's instructional level. For example, the informal reading inventory is probably the most valuable reading test that can be given by the classroom teacher. It is an accurate way to predict a child's instructional, and just as important, frustration level. Given periodically, inventories can be used to measure growth.

Teacher Made Tests

Some teachers negate their perception of the children they teach and put more faith in standardized tests than tests of their own creation. However, there is little doubt that teacher constructed tests and rating charts that take into account individual pupil abilities and progress are the best gauges of academic progress.

Teacher made tests have several points in their favor.

- The teacher controls the time. Tests can be kept short enough to keep the attention of the students.

- Questions can be presented in a form familiar and liked by the pupils. Darkening circles or parallel lines on the answer sheet of a standardized test may "turn off" a student who will respond to completion or matching questions.

- Tests cover subject matter recently taught. Although the students may not like to take the tests they understand the purpose of them.

- If there is good teacher-pupil rapport, the children trust in the fairness of the test.

- The teacher has the latitude to set his own standards. Being generous in acceptance of answers often spurs the student to study harder for subsequent tests.

Despite the advantages of teacher made tests, staff members should be cautioned to use this tool as sparingly as possible. The disadvantaged child is not in his element when called upon to recall information for which he usually has neither the listening nor reading skills to absorb for many minutes at a time, both requiring self-discipline usually lacking in disadvantaged children, and there is little wonder that results are satisfying neither to pupils nor teachers. The teacher who listens closely and observes keenly can believe the commonly heard student comments: "I knew the answers but I couldn't put it down on paper."

It bears repeating to say that tests of all kinds form only one part of the student's progress picture. Motivation, interest, day-by-day adjustment, self-concept, and school and social adjustment are all important factors necessary to complete the portrait.

Reporting Standardized Test Results to Parents

Many standardized tests have accompanying graphs, charts, etc., to send home to parents. For the most part, these are ineffective in a deprived area. Parents find them difficult to understand and often misinterpret their meaning.

The principal who depends upon written communication to parents should simplify the explanation and present no more than necessary to give a picture of the child's achievement.

Conferences are by far the best means of reporting test results. Concerned parents can be encouraged to contact the teacher or principal if they wish a detailed explanation.

In the case of teacher made tests, both pupils and parents have a right to know how standards are arrived at and the meaning and weight of daily, unit and semester tests. The teacher can convey this information to students through discussion. Parents can be informed through an information bulletin from particular teachers, or the principal can include this information in his newsletters that go into the homes. There is further opportunity for parents to discuss tests at scheduled parent-teacher conferences.

Pressure to produce a progress report at regular intervals places the teacher and principal in a dilemma. Following the sound educational practice of taking a student where he is performing and moving him at his own pace can present perplexing problems at marking time. How shall Johnny in the sixth grade who is performing at fourth grade level be marked? He is doing well at his ability level, but how can he be given a B when he is two years behind? On the other hand, if he is given a D it will probably kill further motivation. Quite often the solution, less than satisfactory, is a letter grade based on present progress, with an asterisk which explains some place on the card the instructional level on which the grade is based. When Johnny discovers he is doing below grade level work there is a danger that much of his interest and effort will wane. Unsatisfactory as this system may be, it is better than setting a strict grading scale and holding all children to it. Adhering to such a scale for one marking period for 99 upper elementary students produced the following results.

A's	B's	C's	D's	F's
91	153	284	348	217

Such results re-enforced the obvious. Deprived children cannot be evaluated on standards designed for middle-class students.

Holding Grade Conferences with Pupils

Principals and teachers should not assume that students fully understand grades. The often heard expression "I don't know why she gave me that grade" reveals that a large number of children see grades as something in which they have little involvement.

Successful student conferences can be held near or at the end of a reporting period. The immediacy of a report card makes such a conference meaningful and of student interest.

These conferences can be scheduled in a quiet corner of the room while other students are working. A full explanation of each grade should be given. Care should be taken that conferences not become scolding sessions. The child in question has already received a grade for his efforts. If it is less than satisfactory, positive ways for improving should be suggested but stern lectures on shortcomings will spell the end of subsequent successful conferences.

Conferences on grades should be two way communication. The pupil may reveal reasons or unsuspected problems that are affecting his grades. For example, one teacher, baffled by a good student whose grades plummeted, learned first from a conference that the child spent most of the night staying up with his mother who was suffering from cancer.

The most important aspect of a grade conference is that it gives the pupil the message that he *is* involved in the grades that are marked on his report card and that there are sound reasons why some grades are good and others bad.

The mere fact that students feel they have been thought important enough to be consulted about their grades is pleasing to most. Out of these conferences joint plans can be formulated to bring about improvement or continued good progress as the case may be. Among these might be some form of student self-evaluation which is discussed on the following pages.

Using Student Self-Evaluation

Self-evaluation by students in upper elementary grades is one method some teachers use to arrive at a more equitable marking system. Self-evaluation should include a letter rating by the pupil and a written comment stating why he did well or not so well on a given assignment. Sometimes a comment such as the following reveals graphically why students are often unable to do the work they are capable of doing.

> I didn't do good on this assignment. My dad got mad and made us all go to bed without supper. Then I was kicked out of the bed and had to sleep on the floor. I could have done better if I had time to study.

The grade contract has proved effective for some teachers in matching grades to ability and effort of upper elementary students. An example of this might be a social studies assignment on Cuba. If the student wishes to work for a letter of C, there is a list of required work. In order to gain a B, he must fulfill all requirements for the C grade and complete extra work listed under B. For a grade of A, all other requirements would be completed and additional work, usually centered around independent reading and simple research, would be required.

The freedom of choice and the incentive of a better grade for slightly more effort gives this plan built-in motivation.

No student's report card marks should be the full reflection of student self-evaluation. However, if the teacher encourages self-rating, he must give the results consideration and weight on arriving at grades.

The inescapable fact remains that grades are still the symbols of passing or failing.

If the principal and his staff are one in the thinking that disadvantaged students must be taught at their ability levels, failure does not become a sword hanging over the heads of children. The disadvantaged school that does not follow a philosophy of teaching to individual needs is clearly out of step with modern educational thought.

Developing a Promotion Policy

A promotion policy should be an important order of business in every school. If development of the policy is a cooperative venture between the principal and his staff, it is likely there will be a close correlation between promotion philosophy and educational philosophy.

Developing a realistic policy which looks at achievement in respect to ability quickly brings to light several considerations.

- The general consensus of research on retention is that it does not do what it is intended to do.
- Early identification of problems with special efforts to strengthen areas of individual weaknesses and seeking special help for special needs are usually better alternatives than retention.
- Retentions are not the answer for retarded children or those with deep-seated emotional problems.
- Retentions above the third grade in a disadvantaged school are so rarely successful they should not be considered except in prolonged periods of illness which cause excessive absences.
- The nongraded school organization which moves the child along at his own pace appears to be the best antidote to the deadly poison of failure.
- When after careful consideration retention is thought to be the best educational solution, the parents should be convinced that it is thought of as a positive step with hoped for beneficial results.[4]

[4] Morton L. Light and Frederick Robert Wilson, "An Analysis of Retentions June 1959 to June 1967" (Monroe, Michigan, 1968), p. 3. (Mimeographed)

While it may be years before parents are willing to forego report cards, many are learning that parent-teacher conferences are much more effective in evaluating their children's progress.

When properly conducted, this two way street of communication can open up avenues of insight on the part of both parents and teachers. Evaluating a person of mutual interest and concern can develop the partnership idea of education.

Myriad guides for conducting parent-teacher conferences are on the market and principals should make certain that every teacher has a copy. In addition, one or two staff meetings devoted to this important public relations endeavor is time well-spent.

The commonly heard teacher objection to parent-teacher conferences is that parents who most badly need to be seen won't attend. In all but a very few cases, the school can get parents in the building if a concerted effort is made. This, admittedly, takes extra planning and work.

Work on the theory that advertising pays and publicize the special days set aside for conferences. This should include two or three school fliers and newspaper coverage.

Encouraging the children to get Mom and Dad out pays dividends. A project such as a "Success Book" which displays only the child's best work is a technique that causes students to become powerful persuaders.

Parent groups should be asked to help make conference days well-attended. Volunteer groups can set up pools to call parents on conference days and extend a welcome for them to attend (this also serves as a reminder); furnish transportation for those without it; and provide baby sitting where needed.

Some parents think they should schedule conferences only on parent-teacher conference days. The principal should encourage his parents to develop the habit of coming in and talking it over when the need arises.

After all these means have been exhausted and a few parents remain uncontacted, home visits are the answer. Many teachers dread going into a home, fearing they will be unfavorably received. In most cases these fears are completely unfounded. Teachers who regularly make home visits have generally encountered good experiences. These veterans of visitation should be given opportunities to share home visit experiences and suggest effective techniques in order to convince other staff members of its worth.

The most important point of all is to make certain the parent knows in advance of the teacher's visit and has time to prepare for it.

Parents of the disadvantaged child, more likely than not, harbor some unhappy memories of school experiences. Inviting them to school often and treating them as partners in the education of their children can do much to erase these memories and bring about more interest and cooperation.

SUMMARY

It is difficult to obtain valid results from group standardized tests in disadvantaged schools due to the difficulty of finding "culture fair" tests and test alienation which is common to so many disadvantaged students.

Despite doubts of the value of standardized testing with the deprived, assessment is needed.

In establishing a testing program, the opinions of teachers, students and parents should be solicited and considered.

A staff group testing committee is the most effective means of assuring a realistic and sound testing program. Experienced, knowledgeable staff members establish criteria for test selection, analyze the existing testing program, make decisions for revisions and change, and hold in-service training for teachers in administering, interpreting and using test results.

To provide peak performance, the committee should ask for teacher evaluations of their training sessions.

Many factors must be taken into consideration in assessment of disadvantaged children. The home conditions, feelings toward school and teachers, and the belief that the teacher likes or does not like him can greatly influence not only test results but school work as well.

The importance of self-image cannot be overemphasized.

Attempting to grade the disadvantaged student places the teacher and principal in a quandary. Trying to reconcile rating scales to the philosophy of instructing a child at his ability level is often like trying to untie the Gordian Knot.

Every school should develop a promotion policy consistent with its educational philosophy.

Parent-teacher conferences and home visits are effective ways of parent reporting and have plus features of developing a partnership relationship between parent and school and friendly relations between teachers and parents.

7

Initiating Change and Developing Innovative Programs

The principal must be an initiator and innovator. Teachers by virtue of their daily contacts with children and curriculum, are in the best position to make suggestions for program improvement and innovation. However, because they lack time for all the necessary tasks associated with change, authority to establish necessary planning committees and administrative levels, teachers should not be expected to assume leadership for innovation that extends beyond the classroom.

There is also the reluctance and resistance on the part of many to change. Many teachers honestly believe the "old ways are best" and feel they do a better teaching job using methods in which they are knowledgeable and comfortable. Others are fearful of new methods and approaches, afraid they won't be able to master the new. A few resist because they don't want to go to the effort it takes to learn, plan, and implement a new way.

The innovative principal takes for granted he will meet a certain amount of teacher resistance. He lays well-founded plans to overcome objections, gives solid educational reasons why change is necessary and will improve the curriculum, and assures the staff of adequate preparation and time to implement the new.

The principal never *imposes* change. Democratic administration is slow but sure. Unless teachers see a need, meaningful change simply won't come.

Teacher involvement is the key from the first to last step. Staff discussions of student needs and curriculum deficiencies set the stage for change. If teachers are given the flexibility to try new ideas in the classrooms, a climate for change is already established.

Identifying Problem Areas

As referred to in Chapter 2, teacher questionnaires are excellent instruments for identifying problems and need for change. Responses to a questionnaire and the following comments led to the decision to take a closer look at the nongraded organization as a possibility for the writer's school.

1. Allow more freedom for individual activity and learning.
2. Give children more concrete experiences.
3. Give more individual remedial work.
4. Do more project work and fewer textbook exercises.

Establishing a Planning Committee

Once the principal gets things started, there are many other functions he must perform. The most important is to plan or design a blueprint for change. This is not a task he assumes alone. A planning committee composed of principal, teacher representatives, parents, superintendent and a board member is insurance that those directly concerned will be involved in important decisions. These committee members also serve as liaison personnel between the school and association groups. This is highly important for teachers must work with the committee, parents must be kept aware of proposed changes, and the superintendent and board must know of plans that require money and materials and affect public relations.

Plans are carried out one step at a time. Children and curriculum are studied. Both require time and effort and are not to be taken lightly.

Techniques That Aid Innovation

When change is considered, the principal uses all his ingenuity and resources to make certain his teachers gain knowledge about the new in every possible way. Current literature and research are made available. Visits to schools with successful programs are one of the best selling methods. One teacher, after visiting a nongraded school, said on her return: "Get me a stump. I want to tell everybody how much better the nongraded would be for our kids."

Seminars and workshops are excellent ways to give teachers the understanding necessary for successfully launching a new program. A workshop, offering college credit, was successfully used by the writer to give his staff a thorough look at the nongraded approach and its possibilities for our deprived pupils.

The staff was agreed that the "lock-step" curriculum and forced pacing were not meeting the abilities and needs of our children. They were looking for a pupil-centered program which allowed for and encouraged individual rates of learning. The nongraded organization seemed to be a long step in this direction.

The workshop sought to identify the particular characteristics and needs of our children and to develop a nongraded program tailored to match these particular needs.

The workshop was short on lectures and long on active teacher participation. Small committees were established to explore five important areas of school operation. The committees and their specific charges follow.

Investigative Committees for the Nongraded School

I. *GROUPING*
   a. Pupil organization
   b. Physical facilities available, limitations of size, etc.
   c. Purposes: skills, activities, discussion, etc.
   d. When? How often?
   e. Basis for groups: academic skills such as language arts, math, and/or social skills
   f. Move to other teachers for various subjects
   g. Size: dependent upon experience provided

II. *PERSONNEL*
   a. Parent involvement: resources, clerical aides, chaperones
   b. Teacher utilization: special competencies, team approach?
   c. Involvement of staff
   d. Special personnel: art, gym, music, social worker, crisis teacher, psychologist

III. *EVALUATION*
   a. Instruments: self-concept, attitudes, interests, achievement, psychological
   b. Specification of levels for measurement
   c. Reporting (what about grading?)

IV. *CURRICULUM*
   a. Physical facilities
   b. Availability and involvement of special personnel from a curriculum development standpoint
   c. Materials needed
   d. Equipment needed
   e. Desirable learning experiences
      1. from viewpoint of teachers
      2. from viewpoint of pupils (devise pupil inventory)
      3. from viewpoint of parents (devise parent survey)
   f. Content (organization of?)

V.   *ADMINISTRATIVE*
   a. Scheduling: Forms, records, who will do scheduling?
   b. Testing and assignment of pupils
   c. Assignment of teachers

From time to time these working committees made a report to the staff as a whole. Essential information was also written and distributed by each committee to all staff members.

Following is the outline of an actual committee report.

EVALUATION COMMITTEE REPORT

This committee has addressed the following issues:

1. Why evaluate?
2. What should be evaluated?
3. What is evaluation?
4. How do you evaluate?
5. Who evaluates?

Some tentative conclusions seem to be:

1. What is assessment?

   It is the systematic collection and recording of meaningful, valid and reliable information on children to be used in making educational decisions.

2. Why evaluate?

   To assist in making educational decisions in these areas:
   a. Child
      – level of achievement
      – progress compared with ability level
      – identification of strengths and weaknesses
      – areas needing remediation
   b. Class
      – general level
      – range of ability or skills
      – groups needed
      – distance anticipated to be covered in the year
      – materials needed
      – anticipated ideal class size
   c. Program Effectiveness
      – revisions reduced grouping problems, etc.
      – needs of children met (based on tabulated records)
   d. Reports to Parents
      – accurate information on progress

3. Who evaluates?

   Evaluation should primarily involve the people most directly involved—the teacher and the child. Assistance of a technical nature may come from several sources.

4. What should be evaluated?

We asked members of the group to identify the kinds of information they, as teachers, need to work effectively with children.

They identified these areas:

a. Social/Emotional Development
   - Self-Image
   - Dependency
   - Peer Relationships
   - Authority Relationships
b. Educational Development
   - Reading Level
   - Arithmetic Level
c. Learning or Aptitude Disabilities
   - Language
   - Verbal Reasoning
   - Perceptual
   - Memory Coding
d. General Environmental

5. How do you evaluate?

Evaluation may be done by securing information for teachers in a systematic way, by standardized assessment techniques. For each of the above areas the following methods were discussed.

a. Social/Emotional Development
   - *Teacher Reports*
   - *Tests and Inventories*
b. Educational Development
   - Teacher Reports

For example:

Actual Reading Level (Estimated)	Reader Completed
Readiness–Early	R–E
Readiness–Upper	R–U
PP^1	PP^1
PP^2	PP^2
P^1	P^1
P^2	P^2
1^2	1^2
2^1	2^1
2^2	2^2
•	•
•	•
•	•

        — *Informal Reading Inventories*
        — *Tests* — (e.g.) Durrell-Sullivan
                        Gilmore Oral Reading Test
        — *Arithmetic Skill Inventories*
   c. Learning or Aptitude Disabilities
        — Language
        — Verbal Reasoning   } "Intelligence"
        — Abstract Conceptualization
        — Perpetual
        — Memory, Coding   } Special Diagnostic Tests
   d., e.
        —School Records
6. Present tests used which can be used for classification:
          K — Draw-a-Man
              Metropolitan Readiness Test
          I — Lorge-Thorndike
        III — Lorge-Thorndike
        LV — Stanford Achievement Test
        VI — Stanford Achievement Test

Other tests, such as informal reading inventories, reading tests, etc., can be added with the assistance and guidance of the group testing committee.

Out of the workshop emerged enthusiasm and a desire to probe deeper into the possibilities the nongraded approach appeared to offer. Committees remained active to work on details of grouping personnel, materials and equipment, evaluation, parent reporting, and all the other various things necessary for implementation.

On an experimental basis, it was decided to try the nongraded with a unique type of grouping. Children were divided into four groups.

1. A group with average or above average verbal skills.
2. A group composed of pupils with average or above average perceptual skills and poor verbal skills.
3. A group of "typical" pupils composed mostly of better students.
4. A group of typical pupils containing mostly slower students.

This type of grouping was tried because children with limited verbal and perceptual skills constitute special problems for the classroom teacher. Identifying these pupils and teaching them as a group allows the teacher to concentrate on the use of instructional techniques and materials that have proved successful for remediation.

In this program it was decided that both teacher evaluation and collection of data by outside observers would be used.

A general model for evaluation, which follows, was written and distributed to the teachers involved.

GENERAL MODEL FOR EVALUATION[1]

I.   STATEMENT OF A GOAL.   Write down on paper exactly what you intend to do. If you are running a class in reading, don't say things like "Goal: to improve child's learning skills," or "Goal: to improve child's ability to read"; but rather say "Goal: to improve child's score on the reading test by ten points," or "Goal: to increase the number of words in the child's sight vocabulary by one hundred words."

The way the goal is stated makes a difference in the kind of evaluation procedure selected.

II.   COLLECTION OF DATA.   Write down exactly what kind of data you will have to collect in order to find out whether you reached your goal. If your goal has something to do with ability to read, it is likely you will need to collect data on how well the child reads. If you want to reduce hostility in your group, it is likely you will want to collect data on the number of hostile acts committed before and after the program to reduce hostility is run.

III.   ANALYSIS.   There are many ways of analyzing data. Some people do it by inspection. Most often some form of statistic is used. Averages are calculated, standard deviations are figured, percentages in different categories are calculated, etc. In some cases even more advanced statistics like the t-test, F-test or analysis of variance and covariance are used to find the significance of the difference between average scores for different groups. Again, different kinds of correlation statistics are used to determine to what degree one thing is related to another. The kind of analysis used depends upon the kind of data collected, the sophistication of the design, and the purpose for which the evaluation is being made.

IV.   EVALUATION.   At last we come to the real issue. After the data have been collected and analyzed, a judgment is made. The program either met its goal or it did not meet its goal. The people involved then sit down to determine why things happened as they did. Out of these evaluation conversations come the plans for future trials of the program, future evaluation procedures, and future results.

Specific evaluative procedures were developed for the nongraded program. Teachers involved were as thoroughly orientated in the evaluation process as they had been in every other step leading to the inauguration of the program. Following is a copy of the evaluation design.

[1]Written by Frederick Robert Wilson, Coordinator of Educational Research, Monroe Public Schools, Monroe, Michigan.

EVALUATION OF
VERBALIZER — PERCEPTUALIZER CATEGORIES
FOR THE NONGRADED PROGRAM[2]

A1.   GOAL: To establish four classes satisfying the following criteria:

Class A: Perceptualizers
Class B: Typical children with loading on strong pupils.
Class C: Typical children with loading on weak pupils.
Class D: Verbalizers

A2.   METHOD: Based on performances on the Metropolitan Readiness Test, the Draw-A-Man Test, and Teacher Ratings, children will be grouped, then adjustments will be made for behavioral problems.

A3.   EVALUATION: After the program is underway, a pre-test will be given which will discriminate between perceptualizers and verbalizers and the chi-square statistic will be used to determine whether the groups differ in composition. (They should)

A4.   A positive evaluation of this phase will indicate that further evaluation will be profitable. A negative evaluation should result in either abandonment of the project or regrouping.

B1.   GOAL: To provide instruction for the groups of children consistent with their needs.

B2.   METHOD: Teachers will be selected for teaching of each of these groups on the basis of whether they will be able to satisfy the need criterion of the study. The teacher placed in the class with the perceptualizers will have to give instruction appropriate to children with those strengths and needs while the teacher assigned to the verbalizers will have to give instruction appropriate to them.

B3.   EVALUATION: Expert observers will be employed to collect data by time sampling the teacher behavior over the period of one year. At randomly selected times on randomly selected days each teacher will be observed in her teaching act and rated on the kind of instruction being given.

B4.   A positive evaluation of this phase will indicate that analysis of student data will be meaningful, a negative evaluation will mean that such analysis would be meaningless and a new project should be designed using teachers who can behave appropriately.

C1.   GOAL: To strengthen perceptualizers' verbal skills, to strengthen verbalizers' perceptual skills, and to do so at a rate which exceeds the growth rate of children in the two typical classes.

PROCEDURE: Collect data at the beginning of the program which will indicate where the children are. Collect data at the end of the program which will indicate how far they have come. Compare.

---

[2]Written by Frederick Robert Wilson, Coordinator of Educational Research, Monroe Public Schools, Monroe, Michigan.

METHOD: Pre-test-Post-test comparisons of scores received by children in each group will determine whether the post-test score for a group differs from the pre-test score for that group by a statistically significant amount. (t-Test) If all scores are translated into z-scores, multiple comparison of groups is possible. If at least one of the pre-test instruments is common to all groups, analysis of covariance is possible.

EVALUATION: If there is a statistically significant difference between any group's pre- and post-test scores, it can be said that that group changed by virtue of the program. If there is a statistically significant difference between mean differential scores (pre-test score subtracted from post-test score) for a test given to all groups it can be said that some groups grew faster than other groups. If the F-ratio in an Analysis of Covariance program is significant for a test given to all groups, it can be said that there is a difference between the adjusted post-test mean scores for certain groups. If there is no correlation between the adjusted post-test scores and other data it can be said that the adjusted post-test scores were not influenced by the extraneous variables for which data was collected.

EXTRANEOUS VARIABLES

Extraneous variables are those which have nothing to do with the program you are testing but sometimes get in the way of your results. If you're hoping that your program will affect all children equally irrespective of the child's intelligence, it is necessary to calculate the correlation coefficient between your post-test scores and the child's intelligence to find how they are related. If they are highly correlated, you can suspect your program did not work. However, if they aren't you can then prove that at least that part of your program worked out.

CONCLUSION

In general, when testing a program of any kind, you have to do three things to insure that your program worked: (1) Make sure the kids you are working with are the kind that the program is supposed to work for. (2) Make sure the program is actually being run as advertised; i.e., that you are actually doing in the classroom what you said you ought to be doing. (3) That you have accounted for things that might get in the way and arranged ways of testing to insure that they didn't.

Teachers who were willing and eager to be a part of the experimental program were identified early and thoroughly orientated every step of the way.

Statistical data collected from the program have not been analyzed at this date. However, teacher observations are optimistic and encouraging.

Using prescriptive teaching techniques and materials is apparently leading to quicker remediation. Children appear to like the nongraded approach better and seem happier in an atmosphere geared to their readiness levels. Liking school and school work are no unimportant factors in a disadvantaged school where the drop-out pattern starts to appear from school entrance.

The Importance of Follow-Up

When a new program starts, the work of the principal and his staff does not end, but merely takes a new tack. The planning committee has the continuing functions of tackling problems, evaluating progress, and planning additional and different steps necessary to reach desired goals.

Parental attitude is an important factor in the success or failure of a new program and it pays to keep them informed regularly about the new venture. The following incident is a case in point.

One evening, while visiting a friend, his son brought me a homework problem in modern math and requested my help. The father remarked: "I can't do this crazy stuff. I can't see any need for it. We built the world on the old kind, didn't we?"

Investigation revealed that modern math had been introduced in the school the year before with practically no parent involvement or education. In many homes, no doubt, some benefits of this educational advance were being negated by parental misunderstanding.

Once the die is cast, go all the way with the change. Total commitment is necessary, even to the point of accepting poorer results until the kinks are worked out. This total commitment on the principal's part includes doing everything possible to provide necessary materials, working with the staff on problems, providing continued in-service education, and *encouraging*.

If the principal has done his ground work well the new approach slowly but steadily becomes effective. It is human nature to look for flaws and the principal should not become overly concerned with some doubts if the general opinion is favorable. The following experience is illustrative of this.

Several years ago the writer instituted a cooperative teaching program. In the beginning, there were the expected problems and some teacher concerns. The teachers were heard, helped, and asked to continue for a year. At the end of the year there were still some expressed doubts, so it was announced in a year end staff meeting that the program would be dropped. At the conclusion of the meeting there were wholesale objections. "We don't want to change," was the consensus.

"But I thought there were some serious objections," was my reply.

"Not serious, just a few problems," said one teacher. She added with a grin.

"After all, you didn't expect it to be perfect, did you?"

Innovation begets innovation. When teachers are involved in new programs that work, they are less hesitant and reluctant to try other promising new approaches.

Spurred by government funding, increased consultant services, and greater pressure to find new solutions for old problems, schools across the land are developing new practices to provide better education.

A good number of these center around offering individual help through tutoring. Tutors may be college students, high school students, trained community women and men or older elementary children helping younger. All have the purpose of not only helping students academically, but of changing attitudes and helping to enhance the tutee's self-concept. A tutoring program has been conducted in the writer's schools for the past four years.

THE CROSS-AGE PUPIL TUTORING PROGRAM

The Cross-Age Pupil Tutoring Program is designed to overcome the academic, social and pychological problems which plague the culturally deprived. It has the further purpose of making life in school more pleasant and rewarding.

The program incorporates the results of several research studies dealing with learning and the educationally deprived. One recurring finding of this research has pointed to the poor self-image held by deprived children. The Cross-Age Pupil Tutoring Program has sought to enhance self-concept through cross-age interaction of children from the *same* background. The purpose of the enhancement was to lead to positive academic, social and psychological adjustment.

From its inception, the hypotheses have remained unchanged. They are as follows:

HYPOTHESES OF CROSS-AGE TUTORING PROGRAM

I. Placing culturally deprived older children in the role of teacher tutors and assigning them specific tutorial duties will result in a more positive self-concept as measured by various teacher and pupil ratings, scales and reports.

II. This change in self-concept will increase general academic achievement in those children as measured by standardized achievements tests.

III.   With tutoring and increased personal attention, the achievement of the younger children will increase as measured by standardized achievement tests.

IV.   As a result of improved academic status, attitudes toward school, teachers, parents, older children and peers will improve as measured by various teacher and pupil ratings, scales and reports.

The First Year

The initial project tested these hypotheses with a limited number of participants with a planned increase for subsequent years if the program proved successful.

Ten culturally deprived fifth grade children performing eight months or more below grade level in reading were selected by their classroom teachers, to serve as tutors for ten culturally deprived second grade children, selected by their classroom teachers, who were performing four or more months below grade level.

Tutoring was done in reading only with the assumption that reading improvement would lead to improvement in all other subject areas.

The tutoring sessions were scheduled for three half-hour periods a week.

All tutoring was done in the second grade classroom while the teacher was working with another group. In this manner the second grade teacher could maintain control. She was responsible for all materials used by the tutors in her class. The first five minutes of the tutoring session were spent briefing the tutors, giving specific instructions for materials to be covered that day. The teacher's presence in the classroom also constituted at-the-elbow help when needed.

The actual tutoring covered a period of fourteen weeks. There was a total of 42 contacts between tutors and tutored. During the project the tutoring-tutored combinations were changed three times. This was done to expose both fifth and second graders to more than one partner, to discourage a dependency that might develop, and to cut short any personality conflicts that might arise.

Prior to actual tutoring, orientation and training sessions were held with all participants in the program.

Orientation sessions were held for the tutors and tutored by the school social worker who volunteered to serve in this capacity.

Parent contacts were made by letter explaining the proposed study and anticipated improvements. Parents were encouraged to communicate with the school during the project to relate any changes on the part of their children that they might observe.

Teacher orientation was conducted for those directly involved in the study. Responsibilities were defined. The second grade teacher would be responsible for materials the tutors would use. She would also be responsible for briefing tutors on effective ways to work with children they tutored. The fifth grade teachers were responsible for seeing that tutors did not fall behind in their own class work. They were encouraged to offer advice on effective techniques in working with others. The major task was to emphasize to tutors and peers that selection as a tutor was a signal honor and to continually escalate the idea that giving help has status and reward.

An after-school, bi-weekly meeting was set for the project staff for discussion, evaluation and planning.

The emphasis was on benefits that could accrue, the importance of working together, and how this could be achieved.

During the progress of the project both tutors and tutored met in a half-hour feedback session each week. In these sessions the participants discussed their progress and concerns. In turn, the coordinator gave advice and encouragement where needed.

At the project's conclusion the positive results were far better than anyone had anticipated.

A school and psychological scale, composed of characteristics necessary for school adjustment, showed a statistical difference between before and after administrations.

A questionnarie concerning the pupils' attitudes toward teachers, siblings, peers and adults showed positive change on the second administration.

The academic growth, tested by analysis of variance, was significant at less than the .01 level for both tutors and tutored. Both groups grew at more than eight times their previous rate in reading and more than four times their previous rate on a composite score.

During the project both tutors and tutored grew at a faster rate than their academically superior peers who were not program participants. Equally important with statistical analysis were parent, teacher and student reactions.

Many parents used the experience of the older tutors to help younger siblings at home. They expressed the hope that the program would continue, indicating they would like other children in the family involved.

Teachers of the fifth grade tutors indicated growth on the part of all tutors except one. Common descriptive phrases from teacher observation reports were:

1. Reading skills have increased.
2. More interested.
3. More attentive in class.
4. More self-confidence
5. Now feels he can contribute.

Every fifth grader participant had improved academic grades and all but two improved in conduct.

Second grade teachers saw similar growth in the tutors, noting more self-control, self-respect and willingness to assume responsibility. They saw similar growth in their second graders, progress in reading, more interest, and experienced less discipline problems.

In summation of their tutoring experience, the tutors observed:

1. It made them feel important to be selected as tutors.
2. Older children can teach younger children.
3. Helping younger children helped their own grades.

The second graders concluded:

1. Older children want to help younger children and can.
2. Older children understand younger children and can be their friends.

Subsequent Years

On the basis of the excellent results of the initial project, it was expanded to include all elementary grades, two through six, the following year. The number of children was increased to 188. Sixth graders were selected to tutor third graders and fifth graders continued to tutor second graders.

ESEA Title I funds were secured to hire a full-time remedial reading teacher to coordinate and supervise the program.

There was one significant difference from the first year program. The tutors and tutored children went to a separate room for tutoring sessions rather than to the classrooms of the younger children, with the remedial reading teacher serving as at-the-elbow help and supervisor for the pupil tutors.

It soon became apparent that this was a serious flaw. While year-end test results showed greater academic growth than the children had previously exhibited, they were far short of the spectacular growth recorded in the initial program. There were also less social growth and outward change in the attitudes toward peers and adults.

It was concluded that the key to the Cross-Age Tutoring Program is to send the tutors to the classroom of the children they are tutoring. The enhancement of the tutor's self-concept comes from his relationship with the classroom teacher on a "teacher-to-teacher" basis and the audience respect and admiration of the other children in the tutored child's class.

One hundred and eighty children participated in the program the third year of its operation. One hundred and twenty pupils comprised the experimental group and were actually engaged in tutoring. Sixty children comprised the control group. These pupils took all pre- and post-tests but did not engage in tutoring activities.

A coordinator was hired to work on a two day a week basis. The coordinator was able to work much more closely with teachers than had been possible before.

As in previous years, the participants in the experimental group were enthusiastic about the program and felt they were being helped. The teachers reported improved attitudes toward school, teachers, older children, and peers. Behavior generally improved. Participants were shown in a variety of ways that they held a position of respect and they usually worked to keep that position.

In the fourth year of operation, The Cross-Age Tutoring Program had 160 participants. The number of pupils involved is expected to fluctuate, depending upon the number in need of tutoring experience.

Cautions to Be Observed

For those readers who might wish to start a Cross-Age Pupil Tutoring Program in their own schools, the following important information should be kept in mind.

> The Cross-Age Tutoring Program is designed to redress specific educational deficits. It is an educational prescription to be applied to children who satisfy certain well-specified criteria. The program should be applied to children of normal intelligence, who are functioning at a lower level of achievement than should be expected given their normal intelligence, who are not suffering from serious emotional, physical, perceptual, or medical disturbance, and who are not severe behavioral problems. To choose otherwise loads the deck against success from the outset.[3]

On the other hand, when children fitting these specific criteria are admitted into the program, they usually have an experience similar to the sixth grade tutor who commented: "Everybody likes to be in the tutoring program because it is fun and helps us do better in school."

[3]Frederick Robert Wilson, "Report on the Cross-Age Tutoring Technique Used in a Culturally Deprived Area" (unpublished research report, Monroe, Michigan, 1968). p. 21.

SUMMARY

The principal plays an important role in innovation. He must be prepared to overcome objections to change by presenting sound, educational reasons to his staff. Workable innovative programs result only when the staff is involved from the first to the final step.

Seminars, study of current research and school visitations are effective methods of informing the staff about proposed new programs.

Once a program is in operation, the prime question of whether it is doing what it was designed to do must be answered. Evaluative procedures must be developed to provide this answer and staff members involved must be thoroughly orientated in the evaluation process.

To give a new program a fair chance, total commitment is required by both the principal and his staff.

Government funding and encouragement has been an important factor in the development of innovative programs. Many innovations center around offering individual instruction and individual help.

The Cross-Age Pupil Tutoring Program is an innovative project that seeks to improve deprived pupils' academic work and enhance their self-concept through cross-age interaction of children from the same background. Older children with school problems tutor younger children with school problems.

Based on four years of operation, positive academic growth has resulted. Teachers have observed that participants appear more interested, more attentive, more confident, and have a better attitude toward school and teachers.

The pupil participants have indicated they feel important to be selected and experience fewer discipline problems than in previous years.

8

Developing the Media Center
for the Disadvantaged

Reading represents a hurdle that too many disadvantaged children never clear. The lack of home reading materials is often perpetuated in undersupplied, inappropriate library materials in the schools.

Almost universally, the school drop-out has poor reading skills. He was never "reached" with a program that convinced him reading was a useful and pleasurable tool. Teaching reading is a difficult task in any school. Without the full cooperation of the pupils and a wide variety of stimulating materials, the teacher of the disadvantaged finds his job doubly hard.

The time the administrator spends on planning and working with the library program is time well-spent. A library that is relevant to the needs and interests of the pupils, supplies help and resources for the staff, and serves the school community, increases the effectiveness of the educational program, and plays an important part in school-community relations.

Providing Facilities

Along with many other undesirable physical facilities, a great many schools serving deprived areas have inadequate library quarters. In these schools it becomes an important administrative task to find usable space. In such a situation the principal, librarian, and staff should give their imagination full play. Some schools have found it possible to set up shelving in the halls. Others have used portable shelves on stages and other school areas that are not in constant use. While these measures will fall far short of standards established by library associations, they do provide some services.

When facilities are inadequate, the principal and his staff will plan for appropriate materials within the classrooms. In addition, teachers will be encouraged to make full use of the school system's centralized library service and whatever city and/or county library services that exist.

City and county library systems are cooperative and willing to work with individual schools. Many provide bookmobile visits on a regular basis; times are scheduled for supervised class visits; demonstrations on the use of the library and audiovisual materials are available for teachers and students. The principal can call for help when he needs "library talks" for his staff or parent groups. He can also receive consultation services when he has plans for new library acquisitions or facilities. These services should be considered a godsend to the principal and his staff who cannot provide adequate library services to the student body and should be utilized to their maximum.

Renovating Existing Structures

Often an older building with adequate or no library facilities at all can be renovated to supply them. In the writer's school, three adjoining classrooms had their walls removed and were remodeled into an attractive, functional facility. Such a project is expensive and the possibilities of federal funding should be explored if the school district finds it difficult to provide financing for such an undertaking.

Experienced staff members and a school librarian should be consulted in planning the new facility. Recommendations and standards for libraries have been made by the American Association of School Librarians and various state associations of school librarians. These standards should be followed as closely as possible.

In an environment where starkness and ugliness are accepted facts, pleasant fixtures and furniture are not frills and foolish luxury. A carpet offers a note missing in most homes yet serves the functional purpose of deadening sound and offers an ideal sitting surface for story-telling circles. Light but sturdy furniture, which is easily movable, provides for both large and small group instruction. Pleasant surroundings are often the first reasons for before and after-school visits. And as a veteran school librarian observed:

"Once the students start dropping by, it isn't long before they're browsing in magazines and newspapers. It usually follows that they become regular readers."

The principal and staff who have the opportunity to remodel or start a new library will do well to consider an instructional materials center which combines both library and audiovisual resources. As previously stated in this book, and myriad other publications, A-V materials play a highly important part in educating deprived pupils. Providing printed and A-V materials in the same facility leads to better coordination and better use of both.[1]

Several publications, available from most libraries, contain complete information on how to design an effective instructional materials center.

Selecting Library Personnel

In selecting the person in charge, whether it be a head school librarian or an instructional materials center coordinator, the principal must first look for a person trained in the area who meets certification requirements. However, this is only the first step, for like the classroom teacher, the librarian must understand and accept deprived children. The traditional picture of the stone-faced librarian, frowning and shushing, simply won't fit in a disadvantaged school. Many children come reluctantly to the library. It takes friendly interest to get them to return on their own.

Understanding and acceptance are also necessary for the librarian will be working with individual children and groups both in and out of the library setting. Group instruction in the use of the library, help to small groups and individuals, and telling stories are a few of the activities that place the librarian into direct contact with pupils.

The librarian should be considered part of the educational team and as such must have a knowledge of the school's curriculum and objectives. Once the person is hired, the principal emphasizes the educational role by including the librarian in meetings pertaining to curriculum and placing him on various curriculum and evaluative committees.

The principal will look for qualities which indicate the librarian can work with adults. The fully utilized librarian aids classroom teachers in selection of materials for group and individual projects as well as other consultative helps. The librarian who has problems in the area of human relations effectively blocks study and exploration that extend beyond classroom walls.

[1] Instructional Materials Committee, *The Instructional Materials Center,* Bulletin No. 369 (Lansing, Michigan: Department of Education, 1965), p. 1.

It makes little sense for a school to hire a trained librarian and then tie up his valuable skills with clerical work that most high school pupils can perform. There's no reason for a principal to fall into this "penny wise and pound foolish" trap.

Employment of subprofessional aides is possible under Title I of ESEA. This person or persons can be hired from the school neighborhood and serve as a public relations bonus. Such personnel can effectively label materials, paste, clean and mend books, and perform all the other tasks necessary for a clean and orderly library.

If funds for subprofessionals are unobtainable, the Neighborhood Youth Corps is a possibility. Hiring these young people provides needed money and may help keep them in school. They are quite capable of doing most of the mechanical and some of the clerical work required.

If neither of these groups can be secured, parent volunteers should be considered. In many deprived communities parents effectively serve the libraries a few hours or days a week. There is another advantage to be considered in using parent volunteers in disadvantaged schools. They serve as another channel of communication to the community which so often misunderstands school operation and objectives. Interest in reading is kindled by telling stories.

It is expected the librarian will conduct story-telling sessions on a regular basis. However, one person cannot serve a large school well. A list of stories especially interesting to youngsters can be compiled by the librarian for classroom use. Drama students from the high school and local college are also a source to tap for telling stories, skits, and other dramatizations.

Help by students themselves should not be overlooked. While there are many tasks elementary pupils cannot perform, there are some they can do quite well. Helping in the library is a highly prized assignment for most, and the boost in self-esteem from such a selection has far more value than the aid they provide the librarian.

Selecting Materials

If the materials in the library or instructional materials center are to be used by community and school, it follows that these groups or their representatives should be involved in the selection of these materials. A selection committee, under the chairmanship of the head librarian, should be composed of principal, teachers, and one or more parents representing the school parent organization.

Standards should be set up for all materials purchased. Among these would be suitability for deprived children, reliability and objectivity in presentation, durability and attractiveness.

When possible, examinations of materials should be made prior to purchase, and demonstrations of equipment by company representatives should be requested.

Aims and objectives of the library program keep everyone responsible for selection alert and aware of these responsibilities. As a case in point, an obvious objective would be to provide books that the students could and would read. This objective could be translated into the following action for a school serving the deprived. Buy books of high interest, low difficulty level. Concentrate on action and adventure stories. Include materials representative of different ethnic and cultural groups and their contributions to the American way of life.

The teachers, librarian and principal, by virtue of their knowledge of school needs, will play the major role in materials selection. This is not to say that the opinions of the parents will be ignored. Parents have insights of community feelings that are unknown to even the most perceiving principals and staffs. Controversial materials should not be shunted aside. Providing materials on both sides of a controversial issue allows for critical judgment on the part of students. However, there is always the possibility that some group will propose materials that are entirely unacceptable. If this should occur, principle must be placed above pressure, and the demands denied.

Students should have some voice in selecting their reading material. Some teachers may feel students lack the knowledge to make wise choices. However, it should be borne in mind that while student selections are often frothy in substance, they represent their interest and enjoyment, both necessary prerequisites to more substantive reading.

One way to arouse student interest is to ask each class to propose a list of books they would like to see in the library. While many favorite book titles will be duplicated many times, each student will feel there are some books he picked, a wonderful incentive for visiting the library and taking a book home.

A reading interest survey of older elementary students can reveal what materials students enjoy reading, the extent to which they read outside their textbooks, and what materials are available in their homes.

Such a survey was conducted in the writer's school with the assumption that a positive relationship would exist between good scholastic achievement and extensive reading interests. Conversely, it was felt that the poor achieving pupils would show little interest in reading and would exert little effort to seek materials. The survey is reproduced here.

READING INTEREST SURVEY

1. Do you *like* to read? Yes No
2. How often do you read a newspaper?   every day   seldom
3. Where do you read this newspaper?   at home   library
4. What newspaper do you read?_____
5. Circle the name of your favorite page, or article. Write in spaces 5, 6, or 7, any pages or articles which you read regularly which are not mentioned in items 1–4.
   1. Front page
   2. Comics
   3. Editorial page
   4. Want ads
   5. _____
   6. _____
   7. _____
6. Do you get a paper in your home regularly? Yes No
7. Do you like to read magazines? Yes No
8. Name three magazines

   _____
   _____
   _____

9. Do you have a library card? Yes No
10. Do you have a library book out now? Yes No
11. If you answered yes in number 10, write the name of the book you have in the space below.

    _____

12. Name three books you have read in the last six months.
    1. _____
    2. _____
    3. _____
13. Do you have a bookshelf in your home? Yes No
14. How many books are in your home?
    more than 25 books   less than 25 books
15. Name three books you have in your home.
    1. _____
    2. _____
    3. _____
16. Do you consider these questions to have been too personal? Yes No

An appraisal of the results of this survey was helpful in arriving at some acquisitions suitable to the professed interests of the various groups. More materials to encourage the better students were purchased. More books and magazines relating to sports and mechanics, the overwhelming favorite of boys, were bought. Girls showed a preference for adventure and career stories with girls as the central characters. The lowest group showed little pretense of interest in any kind of material and reemphasized the extent of reading alienation some teachers must face and seek ways to overcome.

Some Final Considerations in Materials Selection

The disadvantaged child does not fit into the middle-class mold. It follows that meaningful library materials in a disadvantaged school will not fit into the mold of the middle-class school.

Audiovisual materials will be regarded as basic, not supplementary. They furnish the concrete, graphic experiences that are often the only means for getting through to some students.

Final consideration for printed materials will be based on such questions as: Will our children be able to read and understand this material? Will they find the characters and situations relevant and interesting enough to start another page after finishing the one before?

The principal of a disadvantaged school must be imaginative and daring in regard to library acquisitions and convey this attitude to his librarian and staff. If he succeeds, aquariums and terrariums won't be regarded as unusual pieces of library equipment. Rock and shell collections can be as readily checked out as books. Mounted butterfly and insect collections, along with varied cocoons, will be available for science study. Pets, from snakes to rabbits, will find a temporary home among Tom Sawyer, Huck Finn and Tarzan. Inexpensive musical instruments can be checked out for a day or a week. And toys, balls, skipping ropes, jacks, and games can be taken home for a weekend or longer.

Extra work will be required to stock them. But the librarian need not worry about adding entomology, zoology, or plays and games to her library science. There are a host of pupils in every school who would deem it a rare privilege to clean an aquarium or pet's cage, or check out a basketball to an eager boy or girl.

And who knows? The day might eventually come when a kid comes in the library with the intention of getting a jump rope and winds up taking a book instead.

Providing for Maximum Library Use

Many factors account for a library's use. How the teachers feel about the library is one. Their feelings are influenced, in part, by the principal's attitude. Lip service from the administrator is not convincing in itself alone. The principal must constantly seek ways to make his staff and librarian a working educational tandem.

There is little danger that familiarity with the library and its contents will breed contempt on the part of the staff. Administrative action in this area involves working with the librarian and staff to make certain that adequate time is scheduled for supervised class and group work. Just as important is the allowance of free time when students are given the opportunity to do interest research, read for pleasure, or just browse around.

To insure maximum use of audiovisual equipment, the principal must make certain staff members know how to operate it. Most elementary staffs are dominated by women, and a large number of females seem to harbor some innate distrust of sprockets and gears and moving parts. Frequent in-service training sessions, which not only demonstrate the use of equipment but allow staff members to operate it under supervision, dispel fears and lead to greater use. This phenomenon is substantiated by the veteran librarian who observed, "I can always expect an increase in use of any materials I demonstrate, even if it concerns the uses of a set of reference materials."

There are numerous ways to stimulate student use of the library. Pleasant surroundings and an interested, helpful librarian have been mentioned as attraction magnets. Keeping the library open before and after regular school hours is another drawing card. One school capitalized on these times by forming two reading clubs, the BSR (Before-School Readers) and ASR (After-School Readers). There was friendly competition between the two groups to see which club could read the greater number of books during the year.

Disadvantaged youngsters, with few possessions to call their own, respond positively to tangible rewards. Library or classroom awards in the form of certificates and books can spur many to read. Principal awards in the form of books have proved successful in some schools. In any system of awards, categories should be defined in such a way that effort as well as ability is recognized.

The attitude of the principal, librarian and teachers toward books and other materials will also influence student use. While time should be devoted to teaching respect and care of books, it should be kept uppermost in mind that a book collecting dust is failing its purpose. In the final analysis, the philosophy should be: It is better to use them and lose them, than not to use them at all. Many school personnel have a great fear that books checked out by some youngsters are on the journey of no return. And while some do end up in mud puddles and others get torn by a baby, most find their way back to the library shelves. In support of this, at the close of a recent school year the librarian reported that 136 library books were missing. The writer thought such a number very reasonable when consideration was given to the fact that this represented a year's use of thousands of books by over 700 pupils. However, an appeal to all students on the next to the last school day resulted in the return of 112 more books.

Encouraging Parent Use

A school serving a disadvantaged area should develop a community outlook. The library is an excellent means by which to offer community service and give neighborhood adults the opportunity to take a closer look at the school.

Library facilities should be publicized through periodic newsletters which give information about available materials and services. One issue might dwell on books and the general topics they cover; another could cover audiovisuals, and so on. Parents should be given an invitation to make use of the facilities and the library should be kept open one or more nights a week to give the invitation more than polite meaning.

The pleasant surroundings and furniture arrangement of a library make it ideal for community organization meetings. Encouraging groups to use the library not only provides a community service but is a smart public relations move.

The librarian should be included on occasional parent-teacher organization meeting agendas. A talk or audiovisual demonstration, followed by a guided tour, is an effective way to inform parents about the library program.

Evaluating the Library Program

Staff, student and community use is one important yardstick in evaluating the library program. If there is steady use by all parties, the library is obviously meeting both school and community needs. However, satisfaction should not be allowed to settle into complacency. The library program, like the rest of the curriculum, should change to meet changing needs.

At this point, the reader may feel the writer has gone overboard on surveys and other forms of evaluation.

In the principal's busy, hurried, and sometimes harried day, the easiest trap to fall into is quick decision making in order to proceed to the next problem. Not only is this trap undemocratic, it is also highly ineffective. It ignores a fundamental fact that those who are deeply involved in a decision should have an awareness and involvement in that decision if it is to be effectively carried out. This is not to say that surveys should supplant training and administrative experience and face-to-face contacts. Surveys are systematic means of arriving at the opinions and feelings of those affected by school organization and action, and, as such, are valuable sources of information which help the administrator arrive at palatable and workable decisions.

There is little danger that the principal will become "survey silly" or use this instrument as an excuse for vacillation. Inherent in the principal's job are numerous routine decisions that must be made daily, and other members of the staff would have neither the time nor inclination to take part in these decisions. On the other hand, when important decisions are in the offing, the best administrative move is to "go to your people." One principal summed up this philosophy when he stated: "When it comes to routine office matters, I ask nobody but myself. When it comes to matters affecting curriculum or community programs, I often propose, but never impose."

A number of ways can be used to take a systematic library evaluation. Asking simple, easily answered questions of students can establish how they perceive the library and how it can be improved in light of their feelings.

An evaluation[2] of 690 elementary children in a disadvantaged school, grades one through six, revealed different ways children use the library, their frequency of use, and why they used it. While there were expected differences among grades and sex, the following reasons, in rank order, rated fairly high with all age levels and both males and females.

1. To check out books to take home.
2. To have a quiet place to do classwork.
3. To use reference books.
4. To look at maps and globes.
5. To read magazines.
6. To sit and think.
7. To look at magazines.

The greatest number of pupils indicated they used the library when their class went. The next greatest use was indicated as before-school, closely followed by after-school, use.

---

[2] Raymond Bottom and Frederick Robert Wilson, "Library Evaluation Report" (Monroe, Michigan, 1968). (Mimeographed)

Frequency of use indicated that about 50 percent of the pupils used the library sometimes of their own volition, while the 25 percent who indicated frequent use were matched by 25 percent who indicated they never went on their own.

Along with use, another question sought to find out how many children were checking books out to take home. The question and results follow:

I take library books home:

All the Time	Sometimes	Once in a While	Never
22%	45%	25%	8%

Children indicated the reasons for taking books home were: (1) because I want to read them—46%; (2) because my teacher wants me to read them—27%; (3) because my parents want me to read them—22%. Five percent failed to respond to this question.

A more thorough evaluation may be asked of teachers. If they feel a time-consuming survey is one more exercise in paper work, they may be unwilling to give it thorough attention. If they can be convinced that the purpose is to provide the best possible services for the students, most will give an honest appraisal.

In addition to routine questions regarding the physical facilities, collection of books and equipment, and the classification and care of library materials, several other important questions should be included. Among these would be the following:

1. Do your students enjoy and look forward to visiting the library?
2. Do you feel the library encourages your pupils to read more?
3. Do you feel the bulk of our materials is suitable for disadvantaged children in its vocabulary level, concept level and approach?
4. Do you feel teacher recommendations are given enough consideration in materials selection?
5. Does the librarian give adequate assistance to students in use of library materials?
6. Does the librarian give adequate assistance to teachers in effective use of library materials?
7. Are pupils encouraged to use library resources independently?
8. Do pupils find adequate study materials in the library?
9. Do pupils find adequate books for recreational reading?
10. Do your pupils feel the library is a useful supplier of study resources and pleasure reading?

Every survey should ask for teacher suggestions to improve service.

When the results are in, the principal and librarian should analyze the results carefully. Both strengths and weaknesses should be noted, and planned action, when feasible, should follow. This action should include the teaching staff as much as possible. Teachers should be informed of results and receive explanations of reasons why suggested improvements are not made when they are economically or otherwise unfeasible. Without such follow-up, subsequent surveys will not receive the honest effort that makes them worthwhile.

SUMMARY

The principal should consider the library an important part of his curriculum related tasks.

When library facilities are inadequate, the principal should encourage his staff to take full advantage of all services offered by the city and/or county library systems.

When renovations are possible and financing is an obstacle, federal funding should be explored as a source. Staff members, as well as the librarian, should be included in planning facilities. When possible, an instructional materials center, combining both printed and audiovisual materials in the same facility, should be considered.

It is important that the librarian understand and accept deprived children and be able to relate and work with them and teachers.

Adequate clerical help should be supplied to the librarian to allow him to function in his trained capacity. Clerical workers could be hired subprofessionals, Neighborhood Youth Corp workers, or parent volunteers.

Materials selection should be made by principal, librarian, staff members and parent representatives. Materials purchased should meet selection standards and the aims and objectives of the library program.

When students are given some voice in the selection of library materials, they are more inclined to use the library. A reading interest survey of students may also influence purchases.

Imagination should be used in stocking a library serving deprived children. Thus, in a community where few personal possessions are the rule, not the exception, toys, games, musical instruments, and pets are not out of the realm of relevancy.

Teacher use of the library may be a reflection of the principal's interest. Maximum use can be secured by an interested, helpful librarian, frequent in-service workshops, and tangible rewards for students who use the library most effectively.

Library services should be established for parents in a deprived community and kept open one or more evenings a week. Community organizations should be invited to use the library as a meeting center.

There should be a systematic plan for evaluating the library program, with the idea that weaknesses will be shown up where possible and changes made to meet changing student needs.

9

Maintaining Realistic Disciplinary Practices

The specter of discipline hangs constantly over the head of the principal of the disadvantaged school. The disrupting elements of fighting, lying, cheating, stealing, defiance, truancy, and refusal to work are problems that must be faced every day.

The principal and teacher will face the full gamut of human problems during the course of the year. The child who has acquired a full vocabulary of four letter words without knowing beginning consonant sounds; the boy who has learned all the tricks of fighting yet doesn't understand the simplest of addition facts; the girl who has learned basic sex knowledge and doesn't realize she should wash her hands before meals—these and myriad others with their varied needs will cross the portals of the principal's office, and he must have some answers.

To maintain effective discipline the principal must develop his own clearly defined philosophy of discipline, establish policies and a system consistent with this philosophy, give the teachers and pupils a part in making realistic rules and carrying them out, and make certain that everyone involved—teachers, students and parents—know what the expectations are.

The Principal's Philosophy

Before the principal can establish an effective system for maintaining discipline, he must be sure in his own mind of what he feels and expects. Half-baked philosophies and ideas won't work, for his "discipline code" will be put to the test every day.

Discipline has as its purposes the development of character and citizenship and the maintenance of order in the school. These objectives cannot be realistically met until the principal and teachers have a clear understanding of slum pupils, parents and the environment that influences them.

To be effective, any program of discipline must first, be preventive, second, remedial, and seldom punitive.

The Principal's Responsibilities

As leader of his building the principal is responsible for its orderly operation. He cannot assume the burden for all disciplinary action—this must be a cooperative effort of all school personnel—but it is the principal's function to set up the machinery to bring about desired pupil behavior.

In seeking to establish a behavioral climate, the principal should examine the expectations of pupils, teachers and parents.

Despite the abundance of literature on parent and pupil hostility toward authority and the Establishment, the majority of parents of disadvantaged children want them to conform, just as the majority of pupils are willing to abide by reasonable regulations and limits. Student and teacher morale depends greatly on the behavioral climate. Students must feel their interests and persons will be protected at school. The majority who conform cannot become the victims of threats, bullying, beatings, extortions and thefts.

Teachers must feel there is a firm and consistent disciplinary code that will help them with fighting, thievery, defiance and disruptive behavior.

Involving Teachers

The cooperation of every teacher is vital in maintaining overall pupil control. The principal cannot leave this area open to misinterpretation and confusion. Teachers should have a strong voice in setting up rules of behavior, but once formed they should be written down, discussed and understood by everyone.

Areas of responsibility should be clearly drawn. What inappropriate behavior should be the responsibility of the teacher and what is serious enough for a trip to the office? Unless this is understood the principal may find his time consumed by handling problems such as:

- getting in the wrong seat
- being in an unauthorized classroom area
- pouting
- making funny faces
- making silly noises

On the other hand, it is very important that teachers know they have the backing of the principal when disciplinary action is taken for a just and good cause. The principal is also obligated to take some action when a child is sent to his office. To do otherwise is to repudiate the judgment of the teacher, and invite lowered morale and less teacher concern for discipline.

There is always an element of risk when the classroom teacher is allowed to apply corporal punishment, and teachers should be fully informed of state laws and policies of the local school district regarding this area of pupil control. If administered in anger, the possibility of injury exists, and a lawsuit can result. A few teachers, but enough to be of concern, may use the paddle, as a first, and not a last resort. If a school gains the reputation as a "paddle factory" it may bring community resentment which affects other areas of the school program.

When corporal punishment is allowed, the principal should carefully spell out in writing for what, how and where it can be done.

A better policy appears to be a visit to the principal's office when a spanking is thought necessary. The principal has the additional levers of immediate parent or special services personnel contact, and the power of suspension if the pupil act has gone wholly beyond the limits of acceptability.

Some teachers feel that their only concern is their classroom and see no reason to attempt to control the behavior of children not assigned to them. If the principal believes that every teacher shares a responsibility in maintaining overall discipline, this should be clearly understood by pupils and teachers alike. Otherwise, there is a risk that pupils from one room may ignore or defy a teacher if reprimanded for improper behavior. The risk is just as great that one teacher may resent another correcting her pupils.

Teachers expect fairness and sharing the load. If the principal establishes a system of duties, he should check to see that everyone is carrying his share of the load. Teachers seldom tattle, but they resent their colleagues who shirk their duty. The principal is resented even more if he fails to insist on compliance. Some teachers, like some children, need to be reminded occasionally to follow the rules. While this may be distasteful to the principal, it is part of his job, and some reminders are better than loss of respect of his staff.

Informing New Personnel

Teachers who face deprived children for the first time must be prepared to be put to the test. Many older pupils have developed, to a high degree, the science of gauging a teacher and then testing him to establish the limits that will be allowed. Consider the overheard comment of a sixth grader after the second day of school. "I figure we can just about have him ready to quit in a month." Unfortunately, the appraisal was all too accurate.

New teachers should know from the start that, in dealing with disadvantaged pupils, they may well make or break themselves in the arena of discipline.

Making the new teacher fully aware of how the deprived child thinks, feels, perceives and acts will be number one on the principal's agenda. Great emphasis should be placed on values—the child's and the teacher's—and how the two can hopefully become compatible, or at least understandable to each other.

Pitfall areas of discipline should be completely covered. In pointing out causes of discipline problems, the fact that teachers themselves, through attitudes and actions, often bring on undesirable behavior, should not be overlooked.

Discussing things that most frequently go wrong in classrooms will save the teacher from falling into a trap of his own making.

Time should be spent on demonstrating how to handle common problems. Teachers expect a principal who is prepared to give them answers, and the administrator who can give effective ways of dealing with the disruptive student or the non-producer gains added stature in the eyes of his staff.

Organization is an important part of good discipline and the principal should lay out a blueprint of how it's done.

Finally, the principal should get down to brass tacks with individual teachers. He knows the "special" problem cases assigned to every room. If the teachers can cope with these, their chances of success with the rest of the class are good. The principal makes certain that each teacher knows his greatest challenges and has a thorough scouting report on how to pitch to them before he starts the teaching season.

Deprived children have multiple problems with multiple causes.

There are often multiple ways of dealing with pupil problems and each teacher should be allowed and encouraged to try methods that he feels will work best for him. However, there are general guidelines that promote good discipline, and the principal should not be hesitant in passing hints similar to the following to his staff.

Guidelines for Good Discipline

- Respect the pupil as an individual—and show it!
- Establish an accepting climate free from criticism for every error.
- "Set up" situations that give individual attention and self-approval.
- Be enthusiastic about what you are doing.
- When you are wrong admit it. (Phony face is not a term that infers respect.)
- Plan! Plan! Plan! Spice up learning with variety.
- Take command early. It's easier to let up than tighten up.
- Recognize that most deprived children have some resentments and antagonisms toward the teacher.
- Try to "talk out" problems.
- Give the child the opportunity to give his side of the story.
- Don't let your own problems get in the way of good discipline.
- Don't back yourself or a child in a corner. Always leave a way out.
- Be calm. Strong reactions breed strong reaction.
- Be consistent consistently.
- Be fair in judgment but firm in enforcement.
- Be a good example. Follow your own rules.

Keeping Disciplinary Records

When a child is sent to the principal's office for disciplinary purposes, there should be a good reason and it should be in writing. There are several reasons for requiring a written referral. For one thing, the teacher must describe the exact nature of the problem. This avoids wasting the principal's time. Otherwise, he may have to spend precious minutes trying to worm the story out of the pupil or go to the teacher's room to check on a purely fictitious account that couldn't possibly be true. Relaying one or two of these accounts to the classroom teacher will also convince him of the necessity of a written referral.

Requiring a written referral also prevents angry, spur-of-the moment banishment to the principal's office by the teacher. When he must take time to set it down in writing, another course of action may occur to him.

Finally, these referrals should be kept and filed by the principal. They form a record that keeps him informed of patterns of student behavior. They may further indicate that certain teachers are in need of help in handling particular kinds of problems.

Just as important as the written referral to the principal, is the principal's written note of disposition to the teacher. This serves as a notice to the teacher that not only has some action been taken, but exactly what that action was. Making the disposition report in duplicate and filing one copy allows the principal to keep track of the discipline measures he has taken in the past with particular children and weigh their effectiveness in bringing about desired change.

A student file is also helpful in arriving at decisions when other school personnel are called on to help and when parent conferences are scheduled.

The Team Approach to Corrective Action

The principal should not be expected, nor is he trained, to handle every kind of behavior problem. He should utilize all school personnel at his disposal in helping problem students.

If he is fortunate enough to have a counselor on his staff, the principal should use him as a strong right arm.

In a large elementary school in a deprived neighborhood, it is not unusual for thirty or more pupils to be sent daily to the principal's office for misbehavior. A large percentage of these cases require personal counseling. Based on past records of the writer's school, less than one out of four of these referrals will be repeaters that require more than a few counseling sessions.

The school psychologist is called in to do psychological testing of children who appear to be in need of help. His diagnosis is often crucial in arriving at decisions for corrective action.

The school social worker works with that most frustrating group to teachers and principals—those children with social and emotional problems.

The principal and teachers should work closely with the other team members and there should be full and open communications among them. Conferences should be arranged periodically to discuss cases under study.

Since the principal is responsible for all decisions made by the team, he may consider himself captain of the team. But he will be playing a foolish game if he does not allow every member to contribute all he is capable of from his background of training and experience.

Getting Pupils Involved

If pupils are given no voice in determining the rules of school, they are inclined to feel that the responsibility of observing the rules does not rest on them.

Student involvement begins and should be encouraged at the classroom level. Room rules can be made by children in the room. Teachers should be encouraged to seek ways of teaching children to work together. Group discussion of class problems, "talking out" angry situations, sharing room responsibilities, and stressing self-control are methods that work.

A Student Council can succeed on the elementary level if the council members are selected by students and are not "hand picked" representatives of the teachers. When Student Councils fail, it is more often the fault of the principal and staff who hold meetings merely for show and do not seriously consider student suggestions. Rather than helping, such treatment creates another barrier between the pupils and adults.

A student handbook is worth the time and effort it takes to produce. It should clearly define acceptable behavior on the school grounds, in the halls, and in the classrooms.

The handbook should be more than a lengthy list of "thou shalt nots." It should also include general information dealing with positive aspects of school operations, such as honor organizations and student awards.

Periodic discussions of the contents of the handbook should be held in upper elementary classrooms. One teacher, noted for the good behavior of her class, explained: "Each week we discuss a new topic for a good citizen and then try to apply it to our daily work and play."

Another teacher, successful over a number of years with deprived children, commented: "Early in the year the class as a whole agrees on behavior we should strive for. When a problem arises we discuss it, the reasons for it, its effect, and what we can do to prevent repetition."

The principal and his staff must assume that any serious breach of conduct or continued behavior problem is of concern to the home as well as the school. The fact that some parents are uncaring and hostile should not prevent home contacts when the need arises. Most parents want their children to do well in school and unpleasant encounters are far in the minority.

However, too often school-home contacts arise only when a problem occurs. If the school works for good will in other areas of community life, the working relationship is on much sounder ground when disciplinary problems rear their heads.

A handbook for parents indicates that the school cares enough to let them know what is going on and desires home cooperation and help. The information in the handbook should be designed to give general information on school operation and supply school policies and regulations. With advance information, many trouble spots relating to school hours, student dress and other problem areas are handled by parents.

Parent conferences should not be taken lightly. Telephone contacts are rarely satisfactory for major problems since they involve only the principal and one parent. As a case in point, the writer is reminded of telephone calls to two parents whose children became involved in a classroom fight. The conflict arose over name-calling.

One parent reacted in this manner. After hearing the details, the mother replied: "Well, what did the other boy call my son?" My answer: "That's not the point, Mrs. Doe. Your child had the recourse of asking for the aid of the teacher or myself. He simply cannot be allowed to start a brawl in the classroom."

A long pause, then the reply: "Well, I tell my children not to take name-calling."

My comment: "Mrs. Doe, can I expect your cooperation in discussing this with your son?"

Her answer, after another long pause, "Yeah, I guess so." Then an abrupt click of the receiver.

The other parent reacted in a completely different manner. He disregarded my request that he discuss the matter with his child, and kept repeating: "I'll take care of him right away." And that he did. The next day his son informed me: "My dad made me feel the fire in his belt."

Neither was the reaction desired.

It is best to arrange a parent conference in school. Both parents should be expected to attend as well as all school personnel involved with the child in question. Comments from a counselor or school social worker can substantiate the teacher's word and rid the parents of the idea that the teacher is "picking" on their child.

A conference should not be called unless school personnel can offer some recommendations designed to bring about improved behavior. By the same token, parents should be asked for their recommendations.

The mere act of sitting down and talking things through often clears up many problems that appear to offer no easy solutions. Many deprived children are experts at manipulating adults. In some cases they have successfully bluffed teachers by threatening: "You had better not do anything to me, or my dad (or mother) will come down here and take care of you." On the other hand, they may be carrying stories home designed to place the teacher in the "bad guy" role. When these avenues are closed, many children face the facts and start to conform.

If for some good reason the parents cannot attend a conference at school, a home conference should be arranged. Before visiting the home, the principal should emphasize to the parents that the conference should be conducted in private and not in earshot of other children, relatives or neighbors.

The one advantage to a home conference is that it gives the principal and teacher the opportunity to make a home appraisal of factors that might be contributing to the child's problems. As an example, one home visit revealed the father to be a tyrant. Beatings, loss of television viewing, and bed without supper were common practices. The child in question was expending his pent up hostility in lashing out at his school peers.

Subsequent conferences were arranged with the school social worker. She worked to develop a more positive image of the child in his father's view. The child's strengths and potential were pointed out. Reasons for the child's behavior were explained and better techniques for handling at home were suggested. In time the home conditions improved and the child's behavior at school improved accordingly.

The parent conference is the best disciplinary measure the principal has at his command. It should not be considered as a last resort, but as a reasonable way of mutually working for the welfare of a given child.

Utilizing a Mothers' Group

Every school serving a disadvantaged neighborhood has a "core group" of discipline problems. Forming a mothers' group of these children, with the purpose of better communicating the school's interest in their children, and helping them to help their children with their adjustment problems can bring about improved behavior. There is a possible further benefit to such a group. As they develop social skills a social action group may evolve. They may expand their horizons to include not only changing things for their own children, but the whole neighborhood as well.

WORKING WITH COMMUNITY AGENCIES

The pupil who will not conform to school rules is usually carrying his nonconformity out into the community. In the case of the older child, fighting, stealing and destructive behavior may constitute more of a problem for the community than the school.

Community agencies are willing and eager to help and the principal should utilize these helps when it appears to be of worth to individuals or groups.

The Big Brothers

The Big Brothers organization is often a help that gets a boy back on the right track. An analysis of student records in any deprived school will disclose a large number of fatherless boys. It is a sad fact that a great number of these boys form a hero worship for the neighborhood toughs and all they stand for. Association with a man of good character is often enough to counter negative neighborhood influences.

There is less need for Big Sisters, but in individual cases they may be the agents who allow girls to develop self-respecting rather than self-defeating modes of behavior.

Police Department Programs

Police Counseling has been used with success in some communities, notably Flint, Michigan. The primary purpose in the school is preventive rather than punitive. Such a program is feasible for funding under Title I of ESEA.

It is well-known by every principal in a deprived area that students have little respect for, and often hate, policemen. "Fuzz" is a word that is spit out, and they see him as an antagonist to be feared, rather than a friend and helper.

The principal who can obtain the services of a police counselor can start a program of police visitation to his classrooms. As a "community helper" the policeman can explain his duties and responsibilities. From time to time the teacher will find opportunities to reinforce these ideas.

A visit to the police department and jail by older students can be worthwhile in giving insights to police operation, protection and the cold finality of incarceration.

Family Service Agencies

Family troubles which erupt in quarreling and violence can send a child to school in an emotional state that, to say the least, is not conducive to learning. When investigation reveals that students' school problems are the direct result of home instability, the principal can work through the school social worker for referral of the parents to Family Service or some other agency which performs counseling services.

ADC and Welfare Agencies

The principal of deprived children should not be surprised at the number of ADC pupils his school contains; he should know. Women in fatherless homes seldom have the management skills to handle their money, and this lack of ability often creates problems for their children. Through acquaintance with these families the principal can often provide forgiveness for book fees and other school costs. When an unexpected financial crisis occurs, he may step in and ask other community organizations for help with clothes or medical care. Too often these families don't know where to go for help and they will suffer in silence, as did one widow without coal in December, rather than seek out help.

On the other hand, there are mothers who abuse their ADC allowances. And the mother who spends her money on liquor or supporting neighborhood men instead of her children should be reported for her indiscretions.

The principal who thinks of these functions as beyond his realm will not serve some of his children as well as he could. In many cases, he must think of the home as an extension of the school and step in and seek help for a family that is unable to find it for itself. It's justifiable if the end result is a child or children who come to school in the proper emotional frame of mind for learning.

Juvenile Court Programs

As early as the fourth grade some children are already familiar with the Juvenile Courts. Since the philosophy of the court is to rehabilitate rather than punish, the young offenders are usually counseled and released. Unfortunately, over a period of time many youths become contemptuous of the law and have little fear of apprehension. They feel they can break the law with impunity. This attitude is typified by one sixth grade boy who bragged: "I've stole seven bicycles already and nothin' ain't never happened to me."

To work with the court the principal should request that one official become a contact person with the school. A system should be devised in which the school and court work together to meet the needs of youth. Regular conferences should be held and the program should be preventive as well as corrective.

A preventive program might be designed to change the image of juvenile authorities. After-school programs, conducted by police assigned to the juvenile division, have proved successful in such areas as Water Safety, Fly Casting, and Archery.

Sponsorship of athletic teams gives deprived youth the opportunity to see law officials in a different light. As one boy discovered, "Our policeman coach ain't no different from that other team and their coach works for a telephone company."

In considering the time spent working with community agencies, the principal should not consider them all extra hours. For the problems solved outside school often prevent them from occurring or recurring in school.

Child Guidance Clincs

> One morning a distraught teacher faced this writer and said: "I don't know whether I can stand Charles another day. He bullies and fights the other children. He rejects everything I say and quarrels with the class. He refuses to do his work and disrupts the class countless times a day. Now as a last straw he's started stealing everything he can get his hands on."

As she realized, the teacher was listing the symptoms of a child with deep-seated emotional problems.

The emotionally disturbed child constitutes a problem that can give the teacher and principal many a worrisome day. "Helping Teacher" rooms serve some of these children, but there are seldom enough rooms to handle all the cases found in a disadvantaged school. Regular methods of disciplinary control are not successful with these troubled children. Other kinds of help are needed, and the principal should work through his school social worker to gain the services of a Child Guidance Clinic.

SOME WORKABLE APPROACHES

Group Counseling

Group counseling, conducted by the school counselor, psychologist, social worker or principal, can help "problem" children understand their own behavior and that of their peers and adults.

Typical of such groups were six boys who were having adjustment problems in their room. The teacher saw them as rowdy and uncooperative and the boys felt the teacher was "picking" on them. By discussing the situation and trying to see their behavior through the eyes of the teacher, they were able to see some of their behavior as disruptive to the learning situation.

The boys were allowed to "gripe" about some of the classroom incidents they did not clearly understand. This opportunity to ventilate usually met their needs and made it possible to return to the classroom and function at an improved level. By learning to "talk things out" rather than "act them out," classroom management was made easier for the teacher.

Adjustment Room Program

The adjustment room serves as a calm harbor for emotional storms. When a pupil's behavior becomes disruptive, defiant or overly aggressive, the adjustment room becomes an outlet for immediate removal from the classroom. When the emotional crisis has passed, the student receives counseling designed to pave his way for readmittance to his classroom. Until he returns, the pupil may also be engaged in study in the subject area from which he was dismissed.

The adjustment room teacher should have a thorough understanding of deprived children and should possess guidance and counseling skills.

Caution should be exercised that the adjustment room not become a catchall for all minor disturbances that can be handled quickly by the classroom teacher. By the same token, the program is not effective in handling emotionally disturbed children who require intensive therapy by teachers trained in the field.

Two way communication between classroom and adjustment room teacher is vital. A simple form, such as that which follows, can be devised. The form should be filled out in duplicate, one copy to be retained by the classroom teacher, the other to the principal for his files.

ASSIGNMENT TO ADJUSTMENT ROOM

Name _____ Date _____

Left Room Number_____ Time_____

Subject Assignment: _____

_____

_____

_____

Time Arrived in Adjustment Room _____
Reason for Referral: Please check.

_____ 1. Refuses to work

_____ 2. Talking

_____ 3. Profanity

_____ 4. Sassing

_____ 5. Fighting

_____ 6. Other (Please indicate or explain below)

Give brief explanation:

Teacher _____

Adjustment Report Evaluation:

Good _____

Fair _____

Poor _____

To Student: Turn both copies in to Adjustment Room Teacher on Arrival.

Repeated referrals to the adjustment room during the same day or for the same deviant behavior are also ineffective. When adjustment room counseling fails, the principal should look for other solutions. However, the adjustment room will be successful in dealing with a great number of pupil problems that arise in the normal conduct of school business in a deprived neighborhood.

Student "Buddy" Approach

Even the worst of the "bad actors" have not alienated themselves completely from peers who choose to conform. The good athlete or the popular leaders are often liked and respected by those who flaunt school rules and authority. In some cases these "better behaved" pupils can be assigned to work with problem cases, reminding and helping them to stay out of trouble. In such an arrangement both parties must be in complete agreement, and an adult should be in close supervision to make certain that too much pressure is not placed on the pupil leader. If a partnership does not appear to be working out, it should be dissolved before it ends in total failure.

Conduct Contracts

Some disciplinary measures fail to bring compliance because they are imposed by adult authority with the pupil having no voice or choice in the matter. A contract, which specifies what actions are unacceptable and the corrective action that will be taken for inappropriate conduct, may help modify undesirable behavior. The contract is signed by all parties concerned—the pupil, teachers, parents and principal. Using this approach, the pupil clearly understands what is unacceptable and what will happen if he goes beyond the limits prescribed for him. Like Red Skeleton's characterization of the "mean widdle kid," he is aware of the consequences if he decides to "do it anyway."

Pupil Self-Evaluation

Every school serving the deprived has a group of pupils who are at constant odds with teachers and peers. When it has been established that such behavior is not due to serious emotional problems, the principal might start a process in which the nonconformist is required to take a look at his own actions.

An oral (preferably) or written evaluation in which the pupil recounts his behavior for the preceding week and the reasons for inappropriate actions may start him to thinking about and facing his problems. The pupil may be asked to suggest disciplinary measures for his breaches of conduct. The trick is to channel these suggestions into positive, constructive avenues rather than negative, demeaning ones. An example of this approach is the boy who suggested that he do custodial work around the school until he paid for a window he had deliberately broken. He did such an excellent job that some staff members hired him to help with yard work on Saturdays. His new found source of spending money and self-respect moved him out of the "problem child" class.

SUMMARY

Effective discipline is dependent upon the principal's own clearly defined philosophy of discipline. Discipline should be preventive and remedial, but rarely punitive.

Student and teacher morale depend on the behavioral climate. They must feel there is a consistent policy that protects them against the unruly and disruptive element.

Areas of responsibility for discipline should be clearly drawn. All teachers should understand what types of behavior they are expected to handle. A written policy covering all aspects of corporal punishment is important in the scheme of discipline. All teachers should be expected to share a common load in discipline and the principal should observe to make certain that each does his part.

Informing new personnel is an important function of the principal. He should make certain new teachers are aware of the values of disadvantaged children and pitfalls to avoid. A list of written guidelines often helps the staff "rookies" get off to a better start.

A two way system of disciplinary records between teachers and the principal avoids misinformation and time-wasting, and helps the principal determine the effectiveness of disciplinary measures with specific cases.

When students are given a voice in determining rules, they are more inclined to accept the responsibility for observing the rules.

Parents should be expected to play a part in helping to maintain good discipline in the school. Parent conferences are usually effective means of modifying undesirable behavior.

The principal should seek out the help of community agencies for students who can benefit from their services.

Punitive measures are rarely effective in bringing about desired change. Approaches that place emphasis on pupil participation and responsibility often bring about insights that result in better school adjustment.

10

Working with the Underprivileged Community

Current literature makes much of the fact that parents of underprivileged children are hostile and apathetic toward the schools. There is no doubt that this is true in most disadvantaged areas. However, the schools must accept a share of the blame for this state of affairs. Few inroads can be made against ingrained hostility or apathy when the major emphasis of school-community relations is placed on asking for millage increases. The comment of one parent illustrates this failure in school-home relationships.

> They're coming around nice-like, asking me to vote yes on the school tax raise. The only other time they talk to me is to tell me how bad my kid acts in school. Hell no, I ain't going to vote yes!

Contrary to the opinions of many, most parents in disadvantaged areas want what is best for their children, and they see the school as important to their children's future success. But the majority believe, or have been led to believe, that education is the function of the school and what happens in school and in the home are independent of each other.

The school must take the first steps to overcome this thinking.

Communication is one means of bringing about better understanding and cooperation. This can be accomplished through written materials, meetings, school visitations, organizations, committees and conferences.

But it must be kept in mind that communication is a two-sided coin, and telling parents is only one side. Parents want to express their own ideas, opinions and protests. Not only must they be allowed this privilege, they must be asked and encouraged to make use of this channel.

Communication alone is not enough. The key to a successful community school program is community participation. As parents participate in planning and project work the general reaction is increased enthusiasm and confidence in their abilities to help. Getting involved brings about a better understanding of school and community needs and an increased willingness to tackle these needs.

A mother who volunteered to serve as a playground aide expanded her activities to collecting clothes for the needy children she saw each day. She commented,

> I never knew before that there were so many children in need and that there was so much I could do for them.

INTERPRETING THE SCHOOL TO THE COMMUNITY

A principal of a disadvantaged school should understand that written communications are the least effective means of interpreting the school to the community. The attrition rate of bulletins sent home by students is fearful. Added to this is the fact that many parents never bother to read school releases. Despite these disadvantages, bulletins and other printed matter are useful and necessary for relaying information to the home. The principal can increase the readership if he will keep a few points in mind.

- Keep the bulletins as brief as possible.
- Keep the language simple and free of educational jargon.
- Employ a friendly tone.
- When possible, make bulletins colorful.
- "Educate" the children to take bulletins home.
- Personalize the message as much as possible.

The following flier, announcing a P.T.A. meeting, utilized many of the above guidelines.

ATTENTION PARENTS AND COMMUNITY FRIENDS
OUR SCHOOL NEEDS YOU!

WHEN:	Now
WHY:	You are needed—your abilities, interests, talents, skills and opinions.
WHEN:	Monday, November 28, 7:30 P.M.
WHERE:	School Auditorium
PURPOSE:	To make our school serve every member of the community from 9 months to 90 years.
SO:	Please attend the P.T.A. meeting.

Newspaper Articles

Principals should heed the hen and learn that it pays to advertise. What appears to be old hat to principals and teachers is often new and fresh to newspaper editors and the community. As a reporter remarked to this writer: "Kids are always good stories."

Pictures of school activities are another excellent means of letting parents know what is going on, and they should be utilized often.

The editor and/or reporters of the community newspaper are important contacts for the principal. Friendly relations and an understanding of what is news can pay off in public relations rewards.

School Information Bulletins

An information bulletin, sent out at the beginning of the school year, provides needed information for parents and eliminates some problems before they arise. These bulletins are not without public relations value, as the following parent comment attests: "It was so thoughtful of you to send out the bulletin. Now we know when the kids will be out of school and can plan our family visits and trips."

Without growing too unwieldy, the following can be included:

- School beginning, lunch and dismissal times.
- School vacations.
- Lunch, milk and book fees.
- School policies in regard to absences and tardiness.
- Suggestions for school wear.
- Grading system and dates report cards are sent home.
- Homework philosophy.
- The school telephone number.

Parent and student handbooks, which were discussed in Chapter 9, also allow the parent to gain first hand knowledge of school rules and activities, a much better means than second hand information acquired from the student.

School Visitations

Days set aside for community visitations are excellent opportunities to make public relations hay in the sunshine of good will that usually permeates such occasions. There's nothing wrong in putting the school's best foot forward, but at the same time it should be kept in mind that the school belongs to the people and needs should not be swept out of sight. Indeed, the best means of getting support for school needs is for the parents to view it first hand.

A supply of pass out tip sheets, listing things for the parents to look for, can make their visit more enjoyable and worthwhile. This is an excellent means of highlighting desirable aspects of the program and pinpointing areas where community help could be used.

One principal has utilized this approach over the years to persuade community groups to provide playground equipment for his once pitifully barren play area.

In advance bulletins the principal should tell parents where he can be located on conference or visitation days. Visitors should be encouraged to drop by and discuss school matters of interest or concern to them.

In the majority of homes, parents usually view the school through the eyes of the child. Objectivity is not the forte of the typical elementary pupil, to say the least. The lens of the camera can be quite revealing to parents. The principal or someone on his staff should become a dedicated shutterbug, snapping the everyday activities of pupils as well as the special programs and projects.

A slide presentation in some well-traveled area during school visitations is guaranteed to attract a steady and interested parent audience.

Parent-Teacher Conferences

Despite teacher complaints that "the parents I want to see most never show up," conferences are worthwhile. One way to gain better attendance is to hold conferences immediately after issuance of report cards. Parents are more inclined to want to talk to teachers when good or bad progress reports are fresh on their minds.

A wealth of material is available covering every aspect of parent-teacher conferences and there is little need to repeat it here. However, it is important to remember to keep the atmosphere as informal and relaxed as possible. Make coffee and cookies available at various spots; they encourage spontaneous conversation and friendliness. Get teachers to agree to move from behind their desks when conducting conferences.

If the principal has performed his function, every teacher on his staff will approach conferences with the belief that parents have worthy contributions of their own to make. Parents who leave a conference with the feeling that their ideas were heard and respected can become the influences that persuade those other parents "who never come" that conferences really help and are not a waste of time.

Parent-Principal Conferences

If the principal is to learn the pulse of his people, he must go out among them and learn what they are thinking, feeling and saying. The open door policy should apply to the community as well as the teachers.

Some parents will take advantage of friendly invitations to visit the principal because they want to talk directly with someone in authority when they have a grievance or idea. With other parents it is a prestige factor to talk to the principal. However, the parents who readily come to school to air their views are a distinct minority.

The principal should become acquainted with local organizations and make certain that the leaders know he is available for talks about school matters. It is a wise move to seek to become a member of organizations that serve the community.

The principal should attempt to bring about greater understanding and a coordinated effort of agencies that work in his school community. Community agencies such as the Health Department, Bureau of Social Aid, and State Employment Security Commission can better meet local needs when communication channels are open.

Providing a meeting facility and inviting representatives from the various agencies is usually sufficient to get an agency group organized.

School facilities should be offered as a meeting place for local organizations. The auditorium, gym and kitchen all hold attractions for widely divergent use.

One goal of the community school is to get patrons to think of it as *our* school, and not *their* school. Certainly, widespread use helps engender this kind of thinking.

As valuable as group and organization contacts are, they are not enough in and by themselves. A great number of community people, many of whom are the most bitter and feel they have the least voice, do not belong to any organized group. The best way to make these needed contacts is outside the school on a face-to-face basis. Shopping in local stores provides opportunities for some contacts; short walks through the neighborhood during pleasant weather is time well-spent. A friendly greeting by name to a parent on the street may be worth 20 written fliers from the principal's office.

The more a principal becomes involved in the life of the community his school serves, the more he will be accepted by the community. The principal who isolates himself inside the school building for an 8 to 4 stint and then drives home "to the right side of the tracks" is not likely to come up with needed solutions to combat the "outside" forces of indifference and hostility which affect the "inside" efforts of pupils and teachers.

Parent Classroom Observations

The parent has only his own classroom experience to draw on in trying to determine what is occurring in his child's classroom. He hears of new methods and new organizational patterns, but he finds it very difficult to understand the changes that have taken place.

The opportunity to observe a classroom in action can be an eye-opener in many ways for parents. If asked in advance without the threat of an unfriendly observer, most teachers are willing to have parents visit their rooms.

One parent, after sitting through a social studies lesson that utilized the overhead projector, exclaimed, "I simply can't believe the difference that machine made in getting those kids interested. I thought machines were a lazy way for the teacher to teach her lessons."

Another parent, at the end of a half day's observation, commented: "Now I can understand why my son is getting some of those grades. He wasted half the morning doing everything but his work."

Both parents gained insights they would have found difficult to accept from a school official. Their reactions are similar to most parents who observe actual teaching situations.

Programs for Parents

Barnum never had a surer attraction than that available to elementary principals. Stage a play or musical program and every child performer is a potential drawing card for proud parents, other family members and friends.

Programs featuring pupil performers are excellent starters for overcoming parent reluctance to visit the school. Parents and friends are not severe critics of children's performances and programs do not have to be elaborate or lengthy. With this in mind, various grades and special subject areas can be encouraged to stage productions.

A class or combined grade program will draw a smaller audience but it offers the opportunity for providing a social hour after the performance. One principal of this writer's acquaintance staged a series of coffee klatches following grade level plays and utilized the contacts he made to revive a long-dead parent organization into new life.

WAYS OF GAINING PARENT PARTICIPATION

The basic premise of the community school can be simply stated that both the school and the community have something worthwhile to offer and each needs the help of the other.

It is well-known that parents of the disadvantaged have a reluctance to become involved in school affairs. The easiest solution is to blame it on apathy and indifference and leave the parents out, rather than search for the real reasons for lack of involvement.

An investigation in one school revealed that many parents did not attend school functions because:

- they had large families and had no resources for babysitting.
- they had no transportation.
- they often mislaid or forgot reminders of meetings.
- they had lack of confidence in talking before large groups.
- they did not feel capable of leading a group or committee when asked.
- officers of organizations were often "school picked" and not the choice of parents.

The principal took the following steps and brought a remarkable revival in parent participation.

- A babysitting service was provided at school on meeting nights. Both parent and student volunteers were utilized.
- A corp of parent and teacher volunteers was formed to provide transportation.
- A block committee was formed to telephone reminders of meetings to parents.
- A teacher volunteered to teach a group a "crash course" in public speaking and group leadership.
- All subsequent nominations for office for school organizations were made from the floor on the date of the election.

One principal, faced with a dying parent organization, took the first logical step and asked some members why they had stopped attending. A mother succintly summed up the reasons for failure. "First of all," she said, "we're being talked to death. It's always you people telling us. And half the times they're things we can't do because our homes ain't like yours."

"The second thing," she added, "is that it ain't even the kind of parent group we want."

The plight of this group revealed the serious error of failing to include parents in both planning and operation.

Asking Parent Opinions

In organizing any school group, there should be a felt need by both staff and parents. It is certainly within the realm of the school to initiate groups, but parents should be convinced of their worth and have a voice in their formation.

A questionnaire, similar to the one below, says, in effect, to parents, "We respect your opinion and we want to hear what you have to say."

> Dear Parent:
>
> We are interested in starting a parent group at our school. There are many activities and projects that could be of real benefit to the school and community when an active parent group is organized.
>
> We want the group to be organized according to your desires and to engage in activities that you want. With this in mind, will you please check one of the boxes below and return to school by your child.
>
> Thank you.
>
> -
>
> _____ I want the traditional parent organization with monthly meetings and planned programs.
>
> _____ I want an organization with elected officers that meets three or four times a year.
>
> _____ I want an informal parent group with no elected officers that meets three or four times a year.
>
> _____ I want separate parent groups organized on lower and upper elementary levels.
>
> _____ I want a separate parent group for each grade level.

Involving Parents in Planning

When parent opinions are requested, the underlying assumption is that parents will be asked to help in bringing their wishes to fruition.

Committees serve a time-honored function in planning and they should not be overlooked in the overall school program. However, committees do not function as well in a disadvantaged area as they do in a middle-class school. Besides the forementioned hesistancy of parents to serve, due to feelings of inadequacy, there is reluctance to tie themselves down for regularly scheduled meetings over an extended period of time, and attendance is spotty due to sickness, shift changes, and various other emergencies not as common to the well-ordered existence of the middle-class family.

Parent-Planning Sessions have been used with success in the writer's school. Parents are personally invited by the principal and staff to attend an evening planning session. All parents meet as a group and the purposes and procedures are outlined. The large group is then divided into smaller sections of about ten people. Each sectional group selects a leader and recorder. The recorder is instructed to record all suggestions and comments that evolve from the parent group. After an hour the small groups return to a central meeting place for a general session of group reports and discussion for future action.

The recorder's list of group suggestions is given to the principal at the conclusion of the meeting for further study and action.

A typical program might ask:

1. What can the staff do to stimulate more community interest in our school?
2. What can the school do to better meet the needs of the community in regard to:
   a. pre-school children
   b. in-school children
   c. adults
   d. senior citizens

Often suggestions and recommendations emerge that do not concern the specific topics under consideration. However, they are of concern and some of the most valuable insights and later courses of action have arisen from these expressed concerns.

To list some examples, the staff gained a new slant on homework when parents repeatedly voiced objections to lengthy assignments. A common objection from the parents was that they had neither the time nor the knowledge to help with some of the work.

Parents did not fit the so-called typical mold of the indifferent poor when they expressed concerns regarding their children's work and behavior habits, teacher attitudes, and ways in which the school might provide activities to keep their children off the streets.

One might argue that these concerns do not represent the concerns of the average poor parent. On the other hand, one could argue from the other premise that the concerns have been there all along and that schools can be faulted for not bringing them to the surface.

One father, who later built beautiful puppet stages for several rooms, probably spoke for a majority when he stated: "This is the first time I've ever been asked to help around school. And I ain't going to help unless I'm asked."

Soliciting Parent Help

Securing the help of parents who have never been asked except during millage campaigns, and who doubt that they have any worthwhile contributions to make, is not an easy task.

A flier, at the beginning of the school year, can alert parents to the fact that the school is actively and seriously seeking help. The example reproduced below has been used in the writer's school.

Dear Parents and Community Friends:

We need your abilities, interests, talents, skills and opinions. We want our school to serve every member of the community from one day old to 90 years old. Right now we need some answers from you. Which of the following groups would you like to work on this year?

1. Improvement for our school. _____
2. Evening activities for adults. _____
3. Activities for senior citizens. _____
4. Teen Club. _____
5. Working as teacher aides. _____
6. Babysitting service during meetings. _____
7. Millage publicity. _____
8. Room parents. _____
9. OTHERS: _____
10. _____

NAME _____
ADDRESS _____
PHONE NUMBER _____

While a flier serves to cover the whole school community, it will bring offers of help only from those most assured of themselves and school oriented.

The most effective means is a personal request from the principal or a staff member. Every community has people of recognized abilities and the community-minded principal makes it his business to know and cultivate these talents.

The writer is aware of two successful, ongoing evening classes in wood carving and guitar which began with doubtful, "Well, I'm not sure I can do it, but I'll try if you think I can."

There is public relations value when the principal and staff members attend hobby and recreational activities as learners. Parents see another side which they fail to discern through the mantle of authority. A staff member who enrolled in a square dancing class remarked, "I had to struggle to learn some of those steps, but I had fun, gained some friends, and by golly, despite my two left feet, I learned to dance!"

Some Guidelines for Using Parent Help

There are many ways to use volunteer help and experienced principals are aware of most of them. However, some cautions should be exercised in using volunteer aides.

Talk to the volunteers and determine their motives for offering to help. Seldom, but often enough to rapidly increase the graying process in a principal's hair, help comes disguised in the person of one with a personal ax to grind.

The principal should carefully size up the aides as to personality types and try to match them with teachers with whom they can be compatible. Many a principal who has ignored this important point has woefully discovered after a few weeks that some teachers and aides were openly clashing with each other. More often, when conflicts arise, the parent will register silent protest by dropping out of the program. Either way disillusionment sets in, talk begins, and parent involvement receives a blow.

Inherent in the use of aides is an orientation program for both aides and teachers.

Orientation should clearly define school goals, explanations of instructional methods, child growth and behavior, and acceptable means of discipline. Understanding allays criticism. The responsibilities and duties of each aide should be carefully delineated. Effective means of establishing a teacher-aide working partnership should be explored.

Finally, time should be scheduled each week for a conference among the teachers, aides and principal. Discussion can clear up misunderstandings, evoke new ideas, encourage careful planning, and keep the principal informed.

Paid Parent Aides

If at all possible, the principal should set up positions such as playground aides and lunchroom supervisors on a paid basis. Besides requiring regular, extended duty, there are unpleasant features of bad weather and pupil control. After the initial enthusiasm, the principal will find waning interest, unexpected emergencies, and personal and family illness depleting his volunteer forces. With pay, always a welcome addition in disadvantaged homes, a cadre of dependable, capable aides can be developed.

Parent Evaluations

Principals who conscientiously involve parents in school programs should not fear, but encourage, parent reactions.

A survey has the advantage of reaching a large number of parents, and, under the cloak of anonymity a parent may reveal dissatisfactions he would not openly state. If the principal and staff regard the survey as an instrument that "sees" the school through parents' eyes, and use it as a basis for strengthening weaknesses, it can be a valuable tool for building better programs.

Surveys similar to the following have been used in the writer's school for this purpose.

PARENT REACTION SURVEY[1]

1. Some people have been able to find out things they wanted to know about school programs. Others have had a hard time finding out the things they wanted to know. Which of these statements apply to you?
   _____ When I want to know something about school, I can never find out what I want to know.
   _____ Sometimes I can find answers to my questions about school programs.
   _____ Most of the time when I want to know things, I can get answers to my questions about school programs.
   _____ I can always find out the things I want to know about the school programs.
2. When I need to know things about the school programs at school, I find that I get the best information by:
   _____ Asking my friends and neighbors.
   _____ Asking my (a) child who goes to school.
   _____ Reading the local newspaper.
   _____ Asking a teacher or principal of the school.
   _____ Don't know.
3. When the new program was set up for this year, I felt that I was:
   _____ Not able to get the information I needed to know what changes were made in the program.
   _____ Only able to get a little information about the new school programs.
   _____ Able to get some information about the new programs, but not as much as I would like to have had.

[1]Frederick Robert Wilson, "Parent Reaction Survey" (Monroe, Michigan). (Mimeographed)

_____ Able to get as much information as I needed to answer my questions about the new program.

4. Some people have felt that the new program for school is a real improvement over the past programs offered for the students. Other people have felt that the new program is no better than what they used to have. How would you rate the new school program?

_____ It is much better than what the children used to have.

_____ It is a little better than what they used to have but it still could be improved a lot.

_____ It really isn't any better than the old program.

_____ The old program was a lot better than this new one.

5. There are many different ways in which a school program could be changed to make it better for the children. In what way(s) would you like to see the program changed for next year?

_____

_____

_____

6. One of the ways people judge the public is by comparing what is going on in the schools now with what they did when they were in school. When compared to the kind of school program you had when you were in school, how do you think the program is doing?

_____ The set-up is much better than the kind of school set-up I had when I was attending the public schools.

_____ The set-up is a little better than what I had when I was in school.

_____ The present set-up is about the same as what I had in school.

_____ The set-up I had when I went to public school was much better than the kinds of things they do at school now.

SUMMARY

Communication is a means of bringing about better understanding and cooperation on the part of parents but it is not enough alone. Community participation is the key to a successful community school program.

Interpreting the school to the community can be done through a variety of written methods. Messages should be brief and free from educational jargon.

Inviting parents to school and school functions can give them insights to school operation and may clear up misconceptions.

Parent-teacher and parent-principal conferences serve the twofold purpose of allowing both parties to share information and cooperatively plan for the child's educational benefit.

If the school is to adequately meet community needs, parents must be included in planning, and to a degree, in its operation.

Parents in a disadvantaged area seldom offer help unless asked by the principal and staff. The poor are not without talents and the principal should make it his business to be aware of his people and their special abilities.

In some cases it pays to look a gift horse in the mouth, and the principal should carefully screen parent volunteers, match those selected with compatible teacher types, and conduct orientation sessions for both aides and teachers.

11

Developing a
Community School Program

In a word, the philosophy of the community school is *involvement*. And involvement should mean active parent participation in school affairs, increased understanding of school programs, better education for children, parents, senior citizens, passage of millage issues, and less destruction of school property.

Gaining involvement is no pushover. Participation comes slowly at first but when parents realize they are being heard—really heard—and their ideas are being used, they become the link between the school and community, making the program known and encouraging their neighbors to take advantage of them.

The following case history illustrates how parent participation developed a community school program that met their needs and wants.

MONROE DOCTRINE: INVOLVEMENT—A CASE HISTORY

When ESEA Title I funds became available, the writer's school in Monroe, Michigan, launched several programs designed to overcome the educational and cultural deficits of the children it served. From the beginning, it was realized that improvement efforts could not stop solely at trying to improve the school program since the child is the product of his total environment. If anticipated results were to be realized, a program serving the total community, from pre-school toddlers to senior citizens, should be designed.

It was felt the key was community involvement. Organize parent groups and let neighborhood leadership emerge from these groups. Listen to their opinions and use their talents and skills to help build programs around their expressed interests, needs and wants. These core groups would then become a liaison between school and community, selling the program and encouraging all the people in the Lincoln School Area to participate in resultant recreational and educational offerings.

Like belling the cat, the first problem was getting people to serve in the core groups. Progress was slow. Written communications met with little response. Telephone calls garnered excuses or promises of participation that failed to materialize. Potential leaders lacked confidence in their abilities and shied away from accepting responsibility.

The conclusion was obvious. The indirect approach wouldn't work. At this juncture a Lincoln staff member observed: "I used to sell encyclopedias. I found the only way to sell books was to knock on doors."

This remark led to the appointment of two remarkable women: One a staff member, the other a parent and dedicated school worker. They were assigned the task of knocking on doors, visiting parents and gaining involvement. The enthusiasm of both was expressed by a letter from the parent to the principal.

"I believe that just as Lincoln School is being made a sort of pilot program for new ideas in education, so also should such a parent group develop into a pilot group to spread the new ideas to the community as a whole and let them know the school wants to serve everyone.

"We are aware that the old ways of looking at life and thinking in general are dying and being replaced by the new. We at Lincoln, who have lived with new ideas and found them good, have a responsibility to pass this knowledge to every corner of the community."

Knocking on doors paid off, and the first meeting was attended by 38 parents and others who represented a cross section of the community.

They came to work. Preliminaries were short. They named themselves "Interested Parents," broke into six groups, elected a chairman of each and tackled their assignments.

At the first meeting they addressed themselves to the question: What can the school do to stimulate more parental interest in Lincoln School?

Personal contact had worked with them and it was suggested that each group member be responsible for contacting five neighbors on his block and urging them to attend school meetings. One man observed: "If we can get them started and they learn what it's all about, they'll be more willing to come." Another wit added: "It's just like kissing. Once you find it's fun you don't want to give it up."

Other suggestions were:

- Provide babysitting service so that parents with small children can attend.
- Establish a Parent Visitation Day whereby parents can visit both the school and individual classes.
- Stimulate student interest and this will, in turn, stimulate parent interest.
- Whenever possible, involve students in school programs and this will spur parent interest.

Excellent response was gained when the groups were asked to propose ways of meeting school needs. Following is a compilation of their suggestions.

How can Lincoln School better meet the needs of:

I. Pre-school children?
    A. A program is needed for pre-kindergarten children in this area, perhaps a year long Head Start class.
    B. Kindergarten children should be allowed to bring friends of theirs who would begin school the following year. This would serve as pre-orientation.
    C. A pre-school story hour should be offered and an attempt should be made to involve their mothers also.

II. In-school children?
    A. After-school tutoring sessions would be helpful for children having academic problems.
    B. After-school recreational activities should be held for later elementary and teens to keep them off the streets.
    C. Parents should be contacted immediately when their children are in any kind of trouble.
    D. Teachers should spend more time visiting homes and getting to know the families. However, home visits should not be made without previously making arrangements with parents.

III. Adults?
    A. Adult educational and recreational classes should be provided. Education that would be helpful to A.D.C. parents so that they can get training and become more independent is especially needed.
    B. Parents who have no children should be encouraged to become active in school affairs.
    C. Parents should be asked to work in school projects. Many have skills they would be happy to teach.
    D. Parents should be given orientation programs in new subjects such as math and ITA.
    E. Parents should be informed at all times as to what is being done and what activities are going on in school.

IV.   Senior Citizens?

    A. Senior citizens should be involved in school programs. This would help them feel needed and also win their favor when millage issues arise.

    B. Most senior citizens have transportation problems. The school should sponsor a weekly program for senior citizens and pick them up with the school bus.

As was expected, the topic of millage created much discussion. Several expressed the view that a school district should ask for the basic amount needed and stick to it. Their opinion: "It shakes voter confidence when a millage amount is decreased to a lower figure after initial defeat." It was a general feeling that particular emphasis should be placed on educating people who have no children as to the benefits they derive from school and to informing non-property owners of their right to vote on millage issues.

One lady commented: "We should keep an active millage committee at all times."

"The school goes to a great deal of trouble forming an organization to get millage passed and then they let it die when the issue is over. We know that millage rolls around as often as influenza so it doesn't make sense to disband a good working organization. In non-millage years work should continue on voter registration and sustained efforts to keep the voters informed on what they're getting for their tax dollars."

The recommendations of the group became a virtual blueprint for a proposal for a Community School Program. The central theme of the proposal was involvement and leadership of people in the community. The proposal suggested that "an adult advisory council should be established to identify current community needs and serve as liaison between school and community."

The blueprint became a reality and Lincoln School became a beehive of activities.

A pre-school story hour was started on Thursday mornings for four-year-olds. American Association of University Women volunteers organized the first programs, but the plan was to relinquish control as soon as neighborhood mothers gained the confidence and skills to take over. Soon the neighborhood mothers were running their show. While pre-schoolers listen to stories or engage in fun activities, their mothers are in another part of the building listening to lectures or observing demonstrations that range from cake decorating to techniques of ironing. Junior high honor students provide babysitting service for mothers with children under four.

Several in-school programs have been added. Over 150 students from grades two through seven stay two afternoons a week for after-school tutoring. The instructors are seniors in the Monroe Branch of Marygrove College.

The after-school recreational-activity program is by far the most popular. Offered one afternoon a week, over 500 children participate. The instructors are 32 juniors from the Monroe Branch of Marygrove College. Activities include: homemaking, charm, arts, woodshop, photography, singing, and various crafts classes. One youngster recently summed by the enthusiasm for this program when he said: "Boy, you guys really knew what you were doing when you started this."

A teen club, with its own officers and regulations, meets one evening a week. A variety of games, from chess to basketball, is available. Frequently dances and skating parties are held. Behavior at Teen Club activities has never been a serious problem and to this date no student has lost his rights of membership.

The school has become a neighborhood center of recreation for both children and adults. In cooperation with the Monroe Recreation Commission, the gymnasium is in use every evening. In addition to organized adult volleyball and basketball leagues, a Slimnastics course is offered once weekly for women. Organized basketball leagues for youngsters are conducted on Saturday.

There are many ways of expressing appreciation. One significant way has been that loss and destruction of equipment have been practically nonexistent.

Several other adult activities of a less strenuous nature are offered in the evenings. Sewing, personal typing and woodworking are popular. Classes are also conducted in modern math and basic adult education. A recent incident graphically points out the favorable attitude of neighborhood residents toward school efforts to serve the total community.

An elderly resident, whose hobbies were furniture upholstering and flower arranging, died. Quite well-to-do, his hobby materials amounted to thousands of dollars, which his sons donated to the school. Commented one: "We like what you're doing for the community and we're happy to be able to help."

In the very near future courses of furniture upholstery and flower arranging will be added to adult activities.

Since the formation of "Interested Parents," a millage issue has come and gone. Using a fan out system that included block workers who were responsible for visiting four or five of their neighbors, every registered voter in the Lincoln area was personally contacted by a worker. The issue carried.

There are favorable reactions to keeping the organization working the full year to promote voter registration and tell the voters what is being done with their tax dollars and the increments they are receiving in turn. There's no reason to believe such an organization won't be successful. Most people commit themselves to issues and organizations in which they are involved.

OPERATING THE COMMUNITY SCHOOL PROGRAM

The beginning is all important when establishing community programs. Skeptics abound and there is great reluctance on the part of adults to become involved in an activity until it proves its worth. The forementioned involvement of parents in planning and offering courses and activities that represent the desires of the community will assure that the program gets off the ground. The care with which plans are laid for actual operation will determine whether the program flies high or falls on its face.

The principal must keep in mind that much of his help will be volunteers. While they will have enthusiasm, and, in some cases, special abilities, they are not teacher trained in the vital areas of instructional methods and human relations.

The principal must anticipate the difficulties they will encounter and prepare them. To do less is to invite disillusionment and a sense of failure.

A brief in-service training period is excellent for volunteer workers. Assigning a "buddy teacher" from the school staff who is willing to answer questions and offer suggestions also helps smooth out rough spots.

Definite decisions as to class size, materials, regulations (which classes will allow adult smoking), discipline for children and all the myriad other details for a successful class must be anticipated and planned in advance.

Despite the most carefully laid plans, problems will arise that have not been anticipated. Most of the problems will be of the situation variety involving one child or a small group of children. Some will be of the here-and-now type that will demand immediate and direct solution. The principal should make certain that everyone knows his whereabouts when activities are in session or the whereabouts of the person designated by him to be available to help in these situations.

Once a program is underway complacency should not set in. People's interests change with time or as their horizons expand. Depending on the specific activity, they might want more time or less, they might want them offered more frequently or less often, and so on. Some system of evaluation and means of determining these changing ideas must be built into the program.

A survey such as that shown in Figure 1 should be distributed periodically, and participants should be encouraged to make their wants known by note or telephone.

Figure 1

COMMUNITY SCHOOL PROGRAM SURVEY

This survey is designed to identify some of the needs and desires of the community area served by Lincoln School with the purpose of operating a Community School Program that serves all citizens ranging from pre-schoolers to Senior Citizens.

Please answer by checking ($\checkmark$).

1. Have you ever taken an evening class?
   ( ) Yes ( ) No
2. Are you interested in adult classes?
   ( ) Yes ( ) No
3. Day preference for adult classes:
   ( ) Monday ( ) Wednesday
   ( ) Tuesday ( ) Thursday
          ( ) Friday
4. Age group of adults: (Check one for each adult in the family)
   ( ) 18-25 ( ) 36-45
   ( ) 26-35 ( ) 45 and over
5. Number of children in the family____
   Name (Husband)_____
      (Wife)_____
   Address _____

Telephone number _____
Occupation (man)_____
Occupation (woman)_____

6. I would be interested in an adult class in one or more of the following categories.
   ___Home   ___Civics-Business
   ___ Hobbies   ___ Amusement
   ___ Academic ___ Art-Music
7. If you have a four-year-old child, are you interested in the school sponsored pre-school story hour offered one day per week for children of this age group? ( ) Yes ( ) No
8. Is your training, knowledge or job experience such that you might be able to teach others?
   ( ) Yes ( ) No
   If yes, indicate area_____

   _____
   (You need not be a H.S. or college graduate to teach, or to assist.)
9. What civic improvement or project would you like to see undertaken in your neighborhood?

   _____

Classes will meet once a week for two hours (7:00 P.M. to 9:00 P.M.) and will span an eight week period.
If ten to twelve people express a desire for a class, the school will offer it, assuming that an instructor can be secured to teach the course.

A survey should substantiate what an observant principal knows. If there are weak areas in the community program, immediate attention should be given to strengthening them. Popular programs should be expanded; unpopular programs dropped. It is extremely difficult to get an adult to stay active, if he has dropped a class or activity for lack of interest or worth.

The Community School Director

A healthy community school program may grow to the extent that the principal is unable to devote the time to it that is needed. When this happy turn of events occurs, the Board of Education will need to consider a Community School Director, either on a part-time or full-time basis, as the need decrees. The principal should be given a voice in the director's employment, since they must be able to work together, and the director will be subject to the principal's authority.

Training and experience in human relations and community leadership should be an important part of the director's background. An open, friendly, understanding personality is also essential, since the director must first sell himself before he sells the program.

EXAMPLES OF COMMUNITY SCHOOL PROGRAMS

A well-rounded community program has planned activities day and night, the year round.

A room, set aside for community use, encourages day activities for groups and offers an excellent meeting place for community clubs.

In-School Programs

In-school programs can be offered to anyone from pre-schoolers to adults. The program that follows, developed from the success of Dr. Samuel Shepard's "Operation Dine-Out" in the Banneker School District of St. Louis, has as its purpose the provision of a dining experience in a restaurant. The expense of this activity is sponsored by Kiwanis and Rotary.

The restaurant dinner culminates extensive classroom instruction designed to acquaint the child with all aspects of dining out. Following is a fifth grade teacher's unit plan of preparation.

ALL ABOUT DINING OUT[1]

I.   Pre-planning
    A. Familiarize teachers with program
    B. Set up tentative schedule
    C. Contact restaurant owners
    D. Contact service organizations for possible financing

II. Enrichment Classes
    A. Developing Self-Image
       1. Good Grooming   Possible Resource People
          a. Cleanliness of: Doctor
             1. Hair   Nurse
             2. Body   Dentist
             3. Teeth
       2. Proper Attire
          a. Clean—both outer and under garments   Clothing Buyers,
          b. Well pressed   both male and
          c. Mended (buttons, etc.)   female
          d. Shoes cleaned and polished   Home Economics
       3. Bus Behavior   Teacher
          a. Getting on and off
          b. En route
       4. Restaurant Behavior
          a. When entering
          b. Checking coats
          c. Being seated
             1. Boys' role
             2. Girls' role
             3. Girls' handbags
          d. Rest rooms
          e. When leaving
       5. Table Manners
          a. Small talk
             1. Across table
             2. To adjacent person
          b. Voice control
          c. Napkins
          d. Table service
          e. Ordering seconds
       6. Ordering
          a. Learning to read menu
          b. Consideration of prices
          c. Cafeteria service
          d. Food selection for balanced diet
    B. Role of the Waitress
       1. Being prompted for special service (personalized)
          a. Special attention toward setting of table
          b. Proper serving

[1]Written by Hazel Belston, Lincoln staff member, Monroe, Michigan.

Pre-school story hour developed out of expressed parent requests that some sort of pre-kindergarten program be organized to help serve as pre-orientation.

The Monroe Branch of the American Association of University Women assumed the task with the understanding that it would be turned over to community mothers as soon as they developed the skills necessary for its continued success. Under the able direction of a former teacher, the program took shape. The following objectives and suggestions to parents indicate the thoroughness with which the program was planned.

PRE-SCHOOL STORY HOUR[2]
Thursday Mornings (10:30-11:30 for Children);
(10:00 for Teachers and Mother Helpers)

1. Objectives
   a. to prepare the children for school
   b. to show them that learning is enjoyable and that reading is fun
   c. to provide social experiences which will help them to fit into a group
   d. to begin development of music appreciation, numbers, and basic science
   e. to learn how to listen, to follow directions, to speak in sentences, and to respect the rights of others
This should be a relaxed, happy hour for both the children and adults present.
2. Suggestions for reading stories:
   a. *Know* the story, pre-read at home aloud.
   b. Interest the children in the story before reading by asking questions or discussing things about it.
   c. Stop during the story occasionally to explain or ask questions, discuss pictures.
   d. Read slowly and clearly.
   e. Ask questions afterwards to encourage good listening habits and to help remember.
3. Suggestions for telling stories:
   a. Know the story, tell it aloud at home first.
   b. Memorize descriptive words, repetition of words.
4. Finger plays, songs, poetry
   a. memorize, use at home.
5. Other suggestions:
   a. There should be fewer than 20 children in a group with 1 teacher to every 8-10 children; 2 adults always present for this number.
   b. When pinning on name tags, greeting at door, and helping children with activities, give them a casual inspection for obvious or contagious illness.

[2]Written by Alice Meyer, AAUW member who supervised development of Lincoln Pre-School Story Hour.

c. Use a kind, confident, quiet voice with the children. Be friendly and interested.

d. Encourage children to say "Good Morning," "Good-bye," "Thank you," "Excuse me," etc., to promote courtesy and good manners. Use good manners for them to imitate.

e. If possible, state directions in a positive form: "Let's" rather than "Don't."

f. Do not try to change behavior by shame. Avoid laughing at a child's efforts.

g. Compare a child with his own progress rather than that of others.

h. Let the child feel he is accepted whether he fails or succeeds.

i. Do not give a choice when you want a definite response.

j. Sit whenever you can to be nearer the child's level.

k. Use simple finger plays or exercises to allow children to change positions during discussion times or story hours.

l. All mothers and teachers should help with the children during rhythms, finger plays, and group discussions.

m. Do not discuss children in their presence: "Isn't he cute?", etc. Do not discuss them outside of school.

n. If children show restlessness or fatigue while listening to a story, stop to ask questions, show a picture, or end it quickly. If children have been sitting too long, have them stand and stretch. Their attention span is *short*! Vary their activity: quiet, active, quiet, etc.

Thank you for your help and please call me when you are unable to come to the story hour.

Mothers of the pre-schoolers were soon deeply involved in the activities of their children. All mothers are required to accompany their children with the idea that many activities can be carried over to the home. Other reasons for this requirement are to allow the parent to gain insights in school expectations; present techniques for creating children's interest; and demonstrate effective methods of controlling children's behavior.

Duties are assigned on a rotating basis. Mothers with no assigned duty meet in the Community Room and receive information on some subject they have requested or engage in some activity in which they have expressed interest.

A typical schedule and assignment sheet for mothers is reproduced below.

PRE-SCHOOL STORY HOUR
Thursday, November 2

10:00   Mothers get out materials and equipment for the children.
10:30-10:45   Activities
   1. At door to welcome mothers and children
      Mrs. M _____
      Mrs. D _____

2. registration of children, addresses, phone numbers
   Mrs. U _____
3. name tages for children—Mrs. P_____ and Mrs. L_____
4. help with coats—Mrs. S_____
5. activities at the tables
   crayons and art work—Mrs. S _____
   Clay—Mrs. M_____
   story books and old magazines—Mrs. H _____
   puzzles and toys—Mrs R _____

10:45-11:05   Music
1. Mrs. U _____starts playing record at 10:45. (clean-up time for five minutes. Each mother helps her table)
2. song with children—Mrs. U _____
3. rythms—directed by Mrs. U _____; all mothers help.

11:05-11:25   Story Hour
Group 1—Mrs. D _____
Group 2—Mrs. M _____
Mothers join one of groups.
1. Discussion of time of year, pumpkin.
2. Poem "The Fall" by Rose Fyleman.
3. Activity exercise.
4. Pumpkin game—What is in the pumpkin?
5. Story of Cinderella.

11:25-11:30   Children put on coats, sit at tables until mothers arrive.
Name tags made by Mrs. P _____, Mrs. L _____, and Mrs. S _____ .

From small beginnings, the attendance in this program has increased fivefold. The majority of mothers have indicated that their children look forward to story hour and are more eager to start school than were older siblings who had no opportunity to attend the program.

New Approaches to Parent Involvement

The Work of Norma Radin and her associates of the School of Social Work at the University of Michigan and Ypsilanti Public Schools holds great promise for those schools who want to move actively in the direction of taking the school into the home and involving the parents in the educative process.

A home counseling program, designed to teach more mothers to teach, has met with good success. Parent workers visit mothers of kindergarten children on a bi-weekly basis with the main objective of helping mothers see themselves as home resources for the child.[3]

Another program, dealing with pre-school children, has as one of its cornerstones a group parent education program, with the twin objectives

[3]Shije Orhan and Norma Radin, "Teaching Mothers to Teach: A Home Counseling Program for Low-Income Parents" (Ypsilanti, Michigan: Ypsilanti Public Schools, 1968), p. 2. (Mimeographed)

of utilizing parents to aid in their children's intellectual development and self-direction.[4]

It has been found in both programs that parents with very limited income can become deeply involved in discussions and activities focused on child-rearing techniques. The research findings show that such involvement results in changes in parental attitudes and practices,[5] and in the case of the kindergarten program, accelerated cognitive development of the child as well.

After-School Programs

The bell that signals school dismissal empties rooms that can be used for as many enrichment activities as available instructors will allow. Art, homemaking, crafts, sewing, photography, chorus, typing, guitar, ballet, story hour, and paddleball offer something for all age ranges and are highly popular with elementary school children.

When classes are scheduled for one hour on a one or two day a week basis, volunteer instructors from the staff and community can be secured to offer a wide enough variety to keep the children participating. The writer's school has had a consistent participation of approximately 600 from a total student body of 900.

Evening Activities for Adults

The preponderence of adult participation will occur in the evening. Cake decoration, typing, knitting, sewing, slimnastics for women, fitness programs for men, woodworking for men and women, and basic adult education courses are some of the most popular offerings.

Trained personnel will be required to teach adult education courses. These should be paid positions. However, course fees should not be expected to pay instructors' salaries. Large fees effectively block participation where finding enough money to pay the rent, and feed and clothe the family is a monumental task. When fees are charged at all, they should be small and be no larger than the amount necessary to cover materials needed in such activities as cake decorating. ESEA Title I funds are available for salaries in most disadvantaged areas where the Board is unable to provide money for this purpose.

[4] Norma Radin, "Piaget, Skinner, and an Intensive Pre-School Program for Lower Class Children and Their Mothers," *Selected Convention Papers: 46 Annual International Convention N.Y.C., April 14-20, 1968* (Washington, D.C.: The Council for Exceptional Children, N.E.A.) p. 59.

[5] Norma Radin and Glorianne Wittes, "Differential Responses to Pre-School Parent Education Program" (Ann Arbor: University of Michigan, 1968), p. 2. (Mimeographed)

When community volunteers are insufficient to offer a wide variety of activities, nearby colleges are excellent sources that should be tapped. Many college juniors and seniors who are majoring in education jump at the opportunity to teach and work with poor parents and pupils.

The gymnasium is an attractive lodestone for neighborhood residents, especially the out-of-school men between the ages of 19 and 30 who are still active enough to participate in sports requiring physical stamina.

Gym use should be scheduled so that different age and sex groups have access to it. Females of all ages are willing to play together in various sports and activities. However, men under 30 are usually interested in fast action sports such as basketball, while older men prefer volleyball and less strenuous games.

Prior to the initiation of basketball sessions for neighborhood youth, the writer's school was broken into repeatedly, and vandalism in the form of broken windows and obscene words on doors and windows was common. Since opening the gym in the evenings, school entries have stopped completely and vandalism has all but disappeared.

One long-time educator, who observed a game between a Negro and white team that had no referee except team members to call infractions, went away shaking his head in disbelief at the harmony and fair play that prevailed.

The principal should bear in mind the babysitting problems that prevail in large families and schedule, when possible, activities and courses for older male and female adults on alternate evenings.

Evening Activities for Pupils

A Pre-Teen Club is an excellent, parent appreciated outlet for older elementary children.

"It gives them things they enjoy doing and keeps them off the streets and out of mischief," is the way one parent put it. Her opinion is shared by a majority of parents who fear the streets and the dark influences they have on their children.

A successful Pre-Teen Club will have its operation directed by pupil officers, will offer a variety of activities, and will involve parents in its planning and operation.

At the beginning of each year a planning session should be held with parents and pupils and a new slate of officers elected. A written invitation, such as the following, and some telephoning is usually sufficient to gain parent participation.

Dear Parent:

A special meeting will be held for parents and fifth and sixth graders in the Lincoln School area. This meeting will be held in the auditorium on Monday, September 30, at 6:30 P.M.

By attending this meeting you will enable us to work with you as parents of older elementary children in planning the activities for our school age community. Without your help, cooperation, and guidance in this matter, it will be most difficult to run a top-notch program for our youth.

Please take this opportunity to show an interest in your child's welfare. We need you to let us know what your ideas are on such matters as time limits, programs, dances, etc.

We will look forward to meeting you!

Sincerely,

When the Club starts operation, parents help chaperone activities and sell refreshments to the students. Profits realized from the sale of refreshments are used to purchase materials, games and equipment for future activities.

Saturday Activities

Weekends are prime times for obtaining parent volunteers. Hiking, fishing and archery give some adults the opportunity to enjoy themselves while teaching kids. Every area has men with unrealized coaching dreams who will supervise team supports.

School facilities should be made available for other desired supervised use. During winter months, especially, movies are highly popular with children and approved by parents.

Eight to four is a meaningless phrase for the school that is truly serving its community. It may sound trite, but the more lights that burn inside the building for community use, the more light is shed on outside attitudes.

SUMMARY

Parent involvement is the important key to a successful community program. Gaining involvement is not easy and must be initiated and persistently pursued by the principal and his staff. Poor parents are aware of their needs, and with direction can help plan school programs to meet their needs and wants.

The principal must anticipate the problems parent volunteers will encounter when working as school aides. Responsibilities, duties and regulations must be carefully delineated.

To keep community participation high, some kind of evaluation must be built into the program and participants should be encouraged to make their ideas known.

A well-rounded community school program uses the school to the maximum. In-school, after-school, evenings, Saturdays and summer—all can be utilized to serve all age levels in the community.

12

Extending the School Program Through Summer

The vast majority of deprived children cannot afford the luxury of a summer vacation free from reading instruction. With a predictable three months of little or no reading, the deficits that exist in spring are certain to have broadened by fall.

There is mounting evidence from across the country that summer projects are among the most successful educational endeavors funded by Title I of the Elementary and Secondary Education Act.

The advantages are many; to name a few:

- Smaller classes can be employed. A pupil-teacher ratio of four or six to one is common.
- Staff members can be carefully screened and hand picked.
- Enjoyable, motivating materials tailored to the needs and interests of individual pupils are available.
- In an informal climate both pupils and teachers gain new insights.
- Teachers have time to individually assess pupils and truly individualize instruction.
- Absence of grades and report cards dispels fear of failure.
- Children have better opportunities for attention, approval and recognition of achievement.

PLANNING THE SUMMER PROGRAM

Summer projects run the gamut from short day camping experiences to sophisticated programs that include reading, recreation and crafts and involve a schedule of three or more hours daily. A program of this scope and size will be considered in this chapter.

Establishing Objectives

The first step in planning the program is to arrive at a set of objectives. These goals not only help in making other decisions, but are usually needed as justification of the program if it is to be funded by ESEA Title I. Some general objectives of summer school would include positive change in participants':

- reading ability
- social skills
- self-concept
- self-control
- attitudes toward teachers and school

The specifics of how some of these goals are to be realized will take careful thought and planning, but from experience, due to the relaxed setting of the program, most attitudinal objectives will be met as a natural change through gaining new perspectives and enjoyment and success in the program. This is graphically illustrated by the remark of one blossoming boy to his teacher. "School ain't supposed to be fun, but this is the best summer I've ever had!"

Deciding Program Details

Finances have the final say and the amount of available funds determines the number of participants and length of the program. It is wise to ascertain as early as possible the exact amount that can be used, for no firm and final plans can be settled until this amount is known.

Once plans are underway, many resources must be tapped to help finalize decisions.

Site Selection

One of the first decisions must concern the site. If program participants are limited to the principal's own school, he must inform his custodial staff far enough in advance for them to plan a work schedule to avoid conflict. In the event the program is to include more than one school, other problems crop up. A satisfactory site must be agreed upon by all school representatives. The site should be as centrally located as possible. There are defensible reasons for moving the program out of the deprived neighborhoods to a school in more pleasant surroundings if the system is comprised of several schools.

Transportation

Transportation becomes a factor when a program serves more than one school. The principal will need the advice and aid of the transportation director when planning bus routes and pick-up points for pupils. Transportation will determine, to an extent, the starting time of the program. If bus routes are long and necessitate lengthy rides for pupils, the program should not begin before 9:30 A.M. Underprivileged children, with their pattern of no set bedtime, simply do not rise early in the morning. If the program is split into morning and afternoon sessions, it is better to schedule younger children for the morning session, since they are more inclined to rise earlier than their older siblings who are allowed more freedom and go to bed later.

Plans should include educating children to bus transportation. Most never ride a bus during the regular school year and have little conception of the importance of reaching pick-up stations on time. The writer is aware of numerous occasions when pupils awakened late and went to the bus stop awaiting a bus that had left an hour or more earlier. Much time must be spent on bus safety and behavior. Many headaches are averted when drivers strong on firmness and understanding are selected.

Food Services

Many sound summer programs begin with breakfast. An appetizing, nutritious meal not only fulfills a health need, but often acts as the spur that gets the child out of bed and on his way to school.

By the same token, an afternoon session has the same solid reasons for starting with a well-balanced meal. Surprisingly, to cooks and teachers, many deprived children are very selective about their food. They prefer to eat the foods to which they are accustomed and are reluctant to try unfamiliar preparations. Seating teachers among the pupils to encourage them to try different foods has been fairly successful for the writer.

Selecting the Staff

When the number of pupil participants has been determined, the search for "the right teachers" should begin. The longer the time to look the better. Every system has well-known "good" teachers who rate highly with colleagues, administrators, pupils and parents. The principal should actively pursue these persons for, as in the regular classroom, the teacher remains the spark that breathes life in the program.

No attempt will be made to list all the qualities of the "good" teacher. However, past experience has shown that successful school teachers must possess patience, understanding and warm friendliness in abundance. The typical child comes to summer school with a negative attitude and a hostility toward strange teachers. If he is experiencing his first summer school, he resents the separation from his friends and the loss of freedom.

Reports are replete with attitudes that changed as the program progressed. This observation by one teacher is typical of many others.

"Ronnie was sulky and uncooperative the first few days. Then a change began and his attitude, desire and personal opinion of himself increased tremendously."

The report of this highly successful teacher could be the blueprint of how to approach disadvantaged children in a summer school setting.

> I simply relax with disadvantaged children. I use what I know about them. Wherever they are, that is where we begin. I believe it is more important for them to have goals and to understand why they must strive, and how they are to strive, than to try to cram knowledge into them.
>
> These children need to know how to solve the problems they understand that they have. This removes the frustration of constant failure and gives them a method of attack. A teacher must help the child learn what his problems are. She must help him find the method of solving his problems. She must make the child aware that he is finding out about himself and that he is using a particular method to solve his particular problems. A teacher should never teach a child a thing unless the child knows why he should learn, and why he should learn a thing in a particular way. In this manner, a child understands, perceives, forms concepts. He is happy in his success. He is competing with himself and as he succeeds, his ego receives a boost.
>
> The program must be structured so that the individual may see his progress. The man who said "Nothing succeeds like success" must have had these kids in mind.

The teacher's instructional approach must be flexible. New methods and new materials are needed catalysts for "failure experienced" children.

Listening, really listening, to the child's ideas, and speaking and thinking in the child's channels can lower the barriers of apathy and change indifference to enthusiasm. When these tactics are employed, it is not surprising that some children who "stood still" during the regular school year show as much as 16 months growth in reading during a five or six week summer program.

As an illustration of the importance of selecting the "right" personnel, consider the reports of two teachers who taught the same children in a summer session. Teacher A saw it this way.

> These students resent authority and want to hurry up and finish things in any old way just to see who is first done. Neatness is meaningless to them.
>
> They argue a lot and exhibit hostility toward each other. Their language is atrocious. They have little respect for school property and equipment. They waste materials and resent the fact that they must clean up their messes at the end of the period.

Teacher B had quite a different view.

> In the short time we were in summer school, I saw many improvements in social attitudes and coordination.
>
> The groups improved a great deal in social attitudes. As they became better acquainted, they found they were able to help each other with their problems; also many children learned to listen better and follow directions. Many improved in using a normal voice when talking in the room, rather than talking unnecessarily loud.
>
> Overall, I found that almost every child was better adjusted to school routine and teachers than he was at the beginning of summer school.

As an alternate plan to seeking the best teachers in the system, the principal might consider selecting from his own staff promising new teachers and others to whom he feels the experience would be helpful. New insights gained from working with smaller numbers should have carryover value to the regular school year program. As one teacher commented: "If this is merely a summer experience that is forgotten in the fall, the program loses half of its value."

Specialists Are Needed

The success formula of few students per teacher works equally well for the specialist.

Speech training will be needed for many of the children. Often the speech teacher enjoys remarkable success as the report of one reading teacher indicates.

One boy had a stuttering problem and was afraid to read orally. The child was assigned to the speech class. In a few days he seemed to have acquired new confidence, and when asked to read orally the stuttering was very slight.

As the program wore on he began to talk to other kids. He remarked often how much he liked summer school.

The speech teacher's reaction: "It's a combination of things. I have time to work with the children. And the relaxed atmosphere, the lack of pressure, and suiting materials to needs releases tension and builds confidence."

In a summer school setting, the school psychologist has time for intensive sessions with referrals. Scheduled times should be reserved for consultation between the psychologist and the staff. An example of the value of the psychologist was a discovery that a large number of younger children possessed perceptual-motor weaknesses. Following his recommendations, methods of developing readiness skills in these areas were incorporated in the program.

One summer school staff member expressed her appreciation for the psychologist's services in this manner.

I wish all teachers could enjoy Mr. F's services in quality and quantity as we have this summer. Many children discovered for the first time that there are adults who will listen and make suggestions without passing judgment.

The health nurse should spend the greatest part of her time making home visits. A complete physical examination for every participant should be basic to the program. It is especially important that thorough vision and hearing tests be conducted. Provision for dental care is also a needed service. Armed with examination results, the nurse has the opportunity to counsel and help parents with their children's health needs.

Preparing the Staff

The depth of experience with disadvantaged children will determine the intensity and extensiveness of staff orientation.

One effective approach is to use experienced summer school personnel to point out expected early behavior and possible solutions. One training session for reading teachers might follow this format.

Problem: Refusal to work.

Possible Solution: Repeat explanations clearly. Encourage, cajole, ignore, try different approaches, but try to avoid a direct confrontation. Above all, persist in efforts to work with child. Some children are testing the teacher. Others fear failure and use refusal as a defense.

Problem: A frequent response to frustration is passivity and dependence.

Possible Solution: Make certain materials are in keeping with the ability levels of the child. Explain thoroughly, but don't do the work. Do not expect too little of these children.

Problem: Children give up easily and find it difficult to remain interested in longer activities.

Possible Solution: Short attention spans are characteristic of deprived children. Vary techniques and approaches. Games, toys, etc. are effective even with older children. Children seek rewards and recognition of a concrete nature. Be liberal in praise, but it must be sincere. Token economy, material rewards of candy, raisins, etc., encourage effort if approriately used.

Other sessions should be devoted to appropriate materials and their effective use.

One approach is the identification of common reading problems at various age levels and development "learning kits" of materials designed to overcome these problems.

If physical education is offered, staff members should know that inattentiveness, unwillingness to compete, poor participation, team effort, and sportsmanship are likely to be apparent at the program's outset.

Allowing children to choose games they like the first few days are good ice-breakers. Later, as the children learn each other and the teacher, behavior, attitudes and participation improve.

Poor coordination is pronounced in many deprived children. A program for coordination development and improvement is a sound educational move, but children least enjoy those activities that demand competence in physical coordination. To sustain interest and participation the program must include the activities participants most enjoy. If it becomes obvious that coordination exercises are killing interest, the program should be ditched in favor of more fun-type activities. One instructor stated this view in a final report.

> Although improvement in coordination was negligible, improvement in behavior and attitudes was considerable. In my opinion, the second far outweighs the first. Twenty years from now it will be of little concern that a child could throw a ball in a target area, but when his ability to get along with peers, competitive spirit, self-control and attitudes improve, much has been accomplished. This has been the greatest contribution of the physical education program this summer.

Arts and crafts instructors will face many of the same problems experienced by reading and physical education teachers with some unique to their own subject area.

Some problems for which they should have prepared answers are:

- "give-up" attitudes toward projects that appear difficult.
- short attention and work spans.
- dependency on teachers.
- rushing through projects with little concern for quality work.
- insistence on taking projects home before completion.
- insistence on starting other projects before present one is completed.
- poor coordination.
- difficulty in following directions.

Clear, simple directions, encouragement, praise, and firm insistence that projects be completed and done to the best of each child's ability are antidotes to most of the above problems. Using this approach results in rapid improvement.

Within a week one teacher reported:

"The children certainly have changed. They start working the second they arrive. Now they are patient with each other, share supplies well, and despite the fact they still want to hurry, they're very proud of the end result."

Children's ages, interest levels, attention spans and coordination skills must be given careful consideration in ordering supplies and deciding on projects.

Following is an example of planned projects for various grade levels used in a five week summer session.

SUMMER SCHOOL ARTS AND CRAFTS

FIRST WEEK

GRADE	5 and 6	Leather billfold kits
	3 and 4	Basket weaving project
	1 and 2	Plaster molds

SECOND WEEK

GRADE	5 and 6	Gravel mosaic
	3 and 4	Weaving yarn project
	1 and 2	Wall panels

THIRD WEEK

GRADE	5 and 6	Construct covered wagons
	3 and 4	Construct birdhouses
	1 and 2	Construct pen and pencil holders

FOURTH WEEK

GRADE	5 and 6	Copper enameling project (pin)
	3 and 4	Stained glass jar and bottle
	1 and 2	Construct sailing sloops

FIFTH WEEK

GRADE	5 and 6	Etch metal trays
	3 and 4	Tineollum block prints
	1 and 2	Weave and trivit

EXTRA FILL INS

100	Stick treasure chests
300	Good grooming kits (leather)
60	Zipper coin purses

Selecting Students

It is no overgeneralization to state that the great majority of children in any disadvantaged school could benefit from a summer school experience. Faced with this fact, the principal must set priorities. While each principal will consider his own situation in deciding who will go, the writer has discovered through trial and error that children meeting these criteria have experienced the greatest successs.

- reading one or more years below grade level.
- emotional stability.
- a tested I.Q. in the 80's or above.

If there are many children who, by necessity, must be left out, the principal has another dilemma to face. Should he concentrate on those with less acute reading problems and hope to bring them up to grade level? Using this approach, he can reserve the regular school year remedial reading classes for those with deeper-seated problems. Or shall he wage a complete attack on the severe problems and hope the less acute cases can muddle through? When this difficult decision must be made, the writer subscribes to the former approach.

Emotional stability is a relative term. Any child from a slum area daily faces problems that build in feelings of fear, hate, hostility, revenge and sorrow. But the great majority are able to adjust and adapt. They will respond to friendly adults who give them kindness, attention, praise and encouragement.

The pupil who is obviously emotionally disturbed can find little help in summer school. The staff will not be trained to handle this child and his problems. Despite the pressures for inclusion that may emanate from classroom teachers, school psychologists and school social workers, the principal should remain firm in his decision.

From experience, the writer has seen little discernible benefits to emotionally disturbed children, but has observed often that these children interfered with learning opportunities of the groups to which they were assigned. This observation has been substantiated by oral and written comments of staff members.

Tested intelligence of disadvantaged children are often misleading predictors of academic achievment. Many factors, as discussed in Chapter 6, account for this. Certainly group test scores should be looked on with caution. Yet such scores do represent a range. Children who are identified as near the retarded range simply won't benefit as much academically as those with more potential. On the other hand, they may gain enormously socially and the principal is faced again with difficult priorities.

Classroom teachers who live, work, and socialize with their children for 180 days a year should know their needs, potentialities and backgrounds better than anyone else. Their opinions are the most valid in the selection process. Information, garnered from the following form, has made the selection process much less difficult for the writer and has furnished valuable insights for the summer school staff.

SUMMER SCHOOL PROGRAM

Child's Name _____ Parent's Name_____
Address _____ Telephone No._____

Last Recorded   Recorded
Reading Score   Present Grade   Intelligence
                                                                 Scores

Word Knowledge _____ _____   _____
Word Discrimination _____

Teacher's Comments

Are the above recorded scores indicative of the child's reading ability? ____
Are the above recorded I.Q. scores indicative of the child's class performance? _____

In your opinion, does this child exhibit characteristics indicative of an auditory or perceptual problem?_____

Is this child emotionally disturbed? _____

Is this child easily frustrated? _____

Does this child give up quickly when frustration level is reached? _____

Has this child been retained previously? _____ Grades _____

Is this child aggressive? _____Withdrawn _____ Neither _____

Does this child have many _____ few_____ no _____ friends?

Does this child participate in games and other activities? _____

_____

Is this child clumsy? _____Well-coordinated?_____

Is this child good _____ Fair _____ Poor _____ in arts and related crafts work? _____

Child's chief area of interest _____

Brief comment on child's attitude toward school, social adjustment, work habits and any other information you feel is pertinent. _____

_____

_____

Brief comment regarding parental concern, interest and cooperation _____

_____

_____

If a choice is deemed necessary as to age and grades, it is probably better to concentrate on younger children for several reasons.

- The reading deficits are not as pronounced in earlier grades.
- Younger children are not in advanced stages of a failure syndrome, and thus are easier to motivate and interest.
- Generally, more outward attitudinal and social changes of a positive nature occur.
- Attendance, essential to success in a short session, is better for younger children.

Parent Orientation

Parent support and acceptance are necessary prerequisites to the success of the program. It is they who must insist the child attends until he learns summer school is fun. It will be their responsibility to see that the child gets out of bed on time and attends regularly.

Soon after the pupil has been selected as a likely beneficiary of a summer school experience, an opening letter, similar to the following, asking parent permission, should go home.

Dear Parent:

Your child has been selected by his teacher as one who would benefit from a Summer Reading Program.

The program will be conducted from July 1 to August 9.

Each session will last three hours. A hot lunch will be served daily. Swimming will be offered one day a week.

The program will consist of reading, arts and crafts, and recreation and physical fitness. There will be no charge for tuition.

We will be unable to determine whether your child will attend in the morning or afternoon until a list of all children is completed. Please do not request that your child attend the Summer School if you intend to go on vacation between July 1 and August 9. The course is so short and concentrated that a few days of non-attendance causes the child to lose most of the benefits that can be derived. Also, it prevents another child, who could attend every day, from being accepted for the program.

Please fill out the form below and return by your child to his teacher by May 15. No child will be accepted for the program after May 15.

Sincerely yours,

. . . .

Please check one:

_____ I DO want my child to attend Summer School from July 1 to August 9.

_____ I DO NOT want my child to attend Summer School.

Child's Name _____

Address _____Telephone Number_____

Grade _____ Teacher_____

_____
Parent's Signature

A series of other letters, fully explaining all aspects of the program, should be sent home periodically. The culminating letter should contain each child's individual schedule and full information about transportation (bus number, pick-up points, times, etc.) if it is provided.

At least one meeting should be held to discuss the program in detail and answer parental questions.

A good public relations move is to write a personal letter of invitation for each parent to attend the program and observe its operation.

An evaluation by the parent is helpful in planning for future programs. The following questionnaire has met with some parent response in the writer's school.

Parent Evaluation

In order to help better evaluate your child, please answer these questions concerning him:

1. What academic changes have you seen?
2. What social changes?
3. What emotional changes?
4. How does your child feel about reading?
5. How does he feel about his teacher?
6. What is your child's greatest problem? Has he received any help this summer?
7. Has he gained self-confidence? If so, explain.
8. Does he tell anything he does in reading at home? What?
9. How do you personally feel concerning his reading?
10. What questions are still unanswered?

Finally, while report cards are anathema to summer school, the parent is entitled to know of his child's progress. A general letter that summarizes the program's activities, and evaluates progress in general terms such as "fair, good, or excellent progress" is sufficient to satisfy parent concern.

A summer program should not become a summer interlude with no planned carryover to the regular program. A prescriptive report, prepared for the child's cumulative folder, should be of real value to future teachers. The principal can make certain summer school reports are read by devoting one meeting in the fall to this subject. The form that follows has been useful in conveying information about summer school participants.

SUMMER SCHOOL PUPIL REPORT

Reading Profile of _____

Comprehension	Pre-test	Post-test
Levels Independent _____		_____
Instructual _____		_____

Identified Areas of Weakness(es):

Identified Areas of Strength:

Approaches that have been successful in teaching this child:

Approaches that have been unsuccessful:

Recommended methods of instruction:

Significant changes in behavior and attitudes:

Materials, equipment and books used in the summer program:

_____
Teacher

SOME ADDITIONAL SUGGESTIONS FOR SUMMER SCHOOL PLANNING

The duration of the term should not exceed eight weeks; in fact, strong consideration should be given to a lesser period. Children need two or three weeks out of the regular school program before summer school begins. At this point many reach a state of boredom and are ready for a fun-type summer experience.

For the same reason, the session should end two or three weeks prior to the opening of school in September.

Class periods should not exceed 35 minute periods. The combination of short attention spans and hot weather make longer periods, as one teacher observed, "lost hectic minutes."

After final pupil selections are made, keep a back-up list. These children can replace program drop-outs and initial enrollees who have second thoughts and fail to show up.

Don't replace drop-outs after the second week. The new enrollee is far behind and upsetting to the program after a few days.

Orientation should be held for participants prior to the end of the regular school term. Emphasizing positive aspects of the program assures good opening attendance.

Another orientation period should be held the first day of summer school. A discussion of program and regulations clears up pupil confusion and uncertainties. This also avoids the headache of non-selected pupils joining the program after the word spreads that it is different and fun.

Lean strongly toward simple, varied and enjoyable activities the first few days. This increases pupil holding power.

Offer activities not found in a normal school setting. Certain times should be scheduled for field trips to points of interest. Recreation should include swimming, hiking, fishing. If funds and transportation are limited, at least one culminating trip or picnic should be planned.

Testing should not be conducted the first three or four days. Test alienation and distrust of strange teachers will cause some to drop out. If possible, it is better that the classroom teachers conduct pre-tests prior to the end of the regular school program. If this is not possible, after a few days when pupils have learned the teachers and the nature of the program, testing can begin.

A team approach works well in testing. One teacher takes two classes while the other individually tests pupils. The advantages are obvious.

Materials should be meaningful, motivating, and enjoyable. Newspapers, magazines, catalogs, word games, listening games, programmed materials, audiovisual materials—all planned to give the disadvantaged child something that he wants to read—should be provided.

Expect a large number of children with perceptual-motor problems and plan accordingly for remediation.

Prescriptive diagnosis, followed by diagnostic teaching, is an excellent method "formula."

When possible, schedule reading before recreation. Strenuous exercise in hot weather tires children and makes attention to reading more difficult.

Carry student insurance. Despite all precautions the strong emphasis on recreation is almost certain to result in some injuries.

Programs Eligible for ESEA Title I Funding

One particular type of program has been described in this chapter. However, so many varied programs of worth to the disadvantaged child can be developed, they are only limited by the imagination and time and personnel necessary to plan and implement them. Without attempting to be inclusive, pre-school, camping, recreation, counseling, cultural enrichment and community programs are some areas that can be funded under ESEA Title I.

Summer School Benefits

Results from across the country substantiate the writer's experience that objectives listed at the beginning of this chapter will be met for a preponderance of the participants.

The children like summer school. They have indicated it numerous times with such statements as:

"I really had fun this summer."

"I've made a lot of new friends."

"I wish summer school would never end."

"I used to not like teachers, but I think they're nice now."

They have proved it in other ways. Children who participate in the program ask to return. Attendance remains high despite heat, vacations, and other conflicting summer attractions.

For evaluative purposes, pre-tests and post-tests have been administered in reading in summer programs supervised by the writer. In three separate programs, composed of over 200 disadvantaged elementary pupils, representing grades two through seven, the following findings resulted.

Summer School	Duration	Reading Gain	
A	6 weeks	Word Recognition	10 months
		Comprehension	5.4 months
B	5 weeks	Word Recognition	9.5 months
		Comprehension	5 months
C	5 weeks	Word Recognition	10 months
		Comprehension	7 months

More importantly, the results have not represented "flash in the pan" gains that were soon lost. Follow-up testing in the fall revealed that most scored as high, and in some cases higher, than their end of summer school scores.

The majority of parents approve of summer school. Many call and ask that their children be included. The following statements, taken directly from the parent evaluation form, reveal favorable viewpoints.

"I have seen general improvement in my son."

"Jane is learning to accept more responsibilities."

"Joe has more confidence to try reading now. He set (sic) down and read me a story the other day."

"Ricky said he liked his teachers. That's the first time I have heard him say that since he was first in school."

"Jim is proud of the things he makes in crafts. Sometimes he talks about his reading. We're proud that he could go this summer."

Staff members, both those who teach in the summer program and those who are recipients of pupil participants, are enthusiastic. Some of the following endorsements have been gleaned from final reports.

"I feel privileged to have worked with these kids this summer. Some insights I gained are priceless."

"I feel the program has been worthwhile and rewarding for students and teachers alike."

"I have seen children start out with a dcfcatist attitude and leave proud of themselves and their accomplishments."

"I have seen remarkable improvement in listening skills and ability to follow directions."

"During the program I observed an increased strengthening of peer relations."

"From the position of positive change in attitude and willingness to participate in group activities, our recreation program was a whopping success!"

"My method of approach has undergone a change. From now on, I shall make a real effort to determine the child's ability. I will not *assume* that he has mastered basic material, but shall really endeavor to discover where he is and proceed from there."

The most cursory examination of these written comments reveals that teachers, as well as students, gain from exposure to summer school.

From the position of one who has supervised four summer programs involving a total of 1,000 pupils, let it be noted that there is much a principal can learn when time and circumstances allow him to work with children where a built-in success factor is the prime ingredient of the program.

SUMMARY

Basic to summer school is a low pupil-teacher ratio which leads to many educational advantages.

The first step in summer school planning should be the establishment of objectives. The principal should seek the advice and help of trained personnel with planning site, transportation and food services.

Time and effort should be expended in making the best possible staff selections. As in the regular program, the teacher is the spark that starts the fire. In addition to classroom teachers, personnel such as a school psychologist, school social worker and a health nurse should be employed to meet pupil needs.

An orientation program that places emphasis on anticipated attitudes and problems and measures that have proven to be effective in countering them assures getting the program off on the right foot.

Pupil selection is a difficult process since the great majority of disadvantaged children can benefit from a summer experience. Priorities favoring those who are likely to benefit most appear to be the soundest educational move. Opinions of classroom teachers should carry the most weight.

Thorough orientation of parents is needed to acquire their cooperation in pupil attendance.

Many varied programs of worth are eligible for ESEA Title I funding.

Summer school benefits are not limited to academic gains. Pupils, teachers and parents gain insights of a positive nature.

13

Using Federal Aid
for Program Improvement

In the past few years so many acts and titles providing financial assistance to education have emanated from Washington that the administrator is often confused trying to keep up with what appears to be the "great numbers game."

The primary purpose of these acts is to improve the quality of education in the nation's schools.

Title I of the Elementary and Secondary Act of 1965 is of particular interest to the principal of a disadvantaged school. This Title provides financial assistance to local schools serving areas with concentrations of children from low-income families with the specific purpose of improving, expanding and initiating programs to meet the special educational needs that are concomitants of poverty.

Despite this clearly stated goal and the massive aid, far too many programs have lacked the imagination and quality necessary to overcome the educational handicaps created by deprivation.

The reasons for failure vary from locale to locale, but it can be generally stated that some of the following "burrs" are present wherever the program machinery has failed its function.

- Failure to include everyone concerned—administrators, staff and community—in planning.
- Hasty planning that places too much emphasis on immediate rather than long-range programs.
- Lack of curricular innovation.

- Watered down programs that attempt to cover too much ground rather than establishing educational priorities.
- Too little direct aid to pupils. Too many funds siphoned off for consultant fees and administrative and clerical salaries.
- Reluctance or refusal of local Boards of Education to provide additional funds to supplement federally financed projects.
- Failure to clearly communicate goals and methods of implementation to participants and public.
- Failure to involve the entire deprived community in programs.

Planning and involvement are insurance against inadequate proposals and programs. The importance and successful examples of community involvement have been covered in Chapter 11. The central place of staff involvement has been discussed also at several points.

Federal programs have made new ideas and rethinking possible. Every administrator and teacher in a disadvantaged school has, at some time or other, fretted at the frustration of inappropriate organizational patterns and materials. When these concerned teachers are given released time for adequate planning and are instructed:

"Look at our situation. Think of our present program and how we can expand, enrich and change it to meet the needs of our children. Give much thought to innovative approaches which you feel might be successful"; ideas and suggestions are certain to result.

The following recommendations emanated from such a group that was charged with developing educational ideas for a program financed by ESEA Title I funds.

TITLE I PLANNING SESSION

Recommendations of Lower Elementary (K-4)

1. Reduce class loads to allow more individual attention.
    a. Maximum of 15-20 in grades one and two
    b. Maximum of 25 in grades three and four
2. Establish a transitional room between kindergarten and first grade.
3. Provide for some sort of pre-school experience. (In-school Head Start)
4. Explore the feasibility of moving towards a nongraded primary.

Recommendations of the Intermediate Group (4-6)

1. Limit class loads to a maximum of 25. (22 preferred)
2. Offer a university extension course(s).
    a. Workshop approach oriented towards needs of the teacher in a disadvantaged school
    b. Course covering discipline, counseling students, utilization of visual aids, drama and the disadvantaged, etc.

3. Provide funds for assembly programs. (as much as $1000)
4. Increase funds for student activities. (Include both field trips and enrichment classes)
5. Offer a summer camping program.
6. Use some Title I funds to hire substitutes so instructors can visit other schools to observe successful techniques, materials and programs.
7. Investigate the possibility of purchasing a video-tape machine.
8. Provide a room for parent conferences and community use.
9. Hire a community School Agent to more fully develop the Community School Program.

These recommendations, along with community suggestions, were incorporated in a proposal.

Writing and Submitting a Proposal

A project proposal is a particular school's plan for the improvement of instruction. Guidelines for the various titles are available from the U.S. Office of Education in Washington. These guidelines give explicit information on priorities, standards, planning, eligibility, limitations, and other pertinent matters necessary for writing an acceptable proposal.

It is good common sense to follow the intent and letter of the law. Yet some school systems have seen the money as a "pot at the end of the rainbow" for pet projects and have experienced problems with attempts to slip through ineligible projects and materials.

Standards should not be regarded as strait jackets but rather as guidelines for building the best possible program. Local administrators should strive to exceed, if anything, federal standards.

In the proposal itself the establishment of need is a key area. The clear exposition of need denotes thorough investigation and establishment of priorities. Project narrative and estimated costs reveal the adequacy of thought and planning that occurred at the community level to meet needs.

Government officials responsible for approval of school projects have definite advice for writing the acceptable proposal. The following suggestions concern Title III of NDEA, which has as a major purpose the acquisition of equipment and materials in various subject matter fields. However, the same factors apply equally well to Title I with its emphasis on programs and related services.

A project application is of greatest value to the Title III staff when it contains not only the necessary fiscal information but also information which will help determine the approvability of the project through an evaluation of factors such as the following:
1. The relationship of the specific project to the school's long-range plan for the improvement of instruction
2. Compliance with State standards, policies, and guidelines

3. The suitability of the equipment to the overall objectives and to its proposed use

4. The ability and readiness of the teachers to use the equipment and materials

5. The feasibility of the local plan for in-service training in the use of the new materials and equipment to be purchased for the project

6. The soundness of the school's plan to evaluate the effectiveness of the project.[1]

For purposes of illustration, an actual Title I proposal follows. A proposal, covering all aspects of the program in the writer's school, is usually in excess of 30 pages. This example, requesting funds for a Community School Program, is sufficient to reveal an acceptable format.

(cover page)

**PROPOSAL FOR COMMUNITY SCHOOL PROGRAM
in LINCOLN - ORCHARD - ST. JOSEPH AREA**

**SUBMITTED BY:
MONROE PUBLIC SCHOOLS
MONROE, MICHIGAN**

"COMMUNITY SCHOOL" PROGRAM

During the past school year, the School District of the City of Monroe made application through the local Office of Economic Opportunity for funding for a comprehensive Community School program fully realizing that any lasting change could only come with total community involvement. Their belief was reinforced by leading authors across the United States.

> One needs only to visit a disadvantaged school to be convinced that the nature of the community largely determines what goes on in the school. Therefore to attempt to divorce the school from the community is to engage in unrealistic thinking that might lead to policies that could wreak havoc with the schools and the community.[2]

Although a number of program improvements have already gone into effect in Lincoln and Orchard Schools, there is still a definite need for further innovations and changes.

> An extended school day and school week (to include field trips to civic, recreational, industrial, and other centers of interest as well as reading clinics, opportunities for recreational reading in the school library, small group academic coaching, and small group guidance) ... will improve the achievement of the culturally deprived in reading and arithmetic, will improve their motivation, and decrease the number who drop out of school before high school graduation.[3]

[1]*NDEA Title III Guidelines*, U.S. Department of Health, Education and Welfare, Office of Education (Washington, D.C.: U.S. Government Printing Office, 1965), p. 35.

[2]James B. Conant, *Slums and Suburbs; A Commentary on Schools in Metropolitan Areas* (New York, N.Y.: McGraw-Hill Book Co., 1961), p. 20.

[3]Frank Riesmann, *The Culturally Deprived Child* (New York, N.Y.: Harper and Row, Inc., 1962), p. 125.

With the reduction in money allocated by Congress to the Office of Economic Opportunity the project did not materialize.

Despite the resultant lack of funds created by the failure of this O.E.O. Proposal, several pilot programs were inaugurated utilizing Title I funds and met with resounding success. These included Teen Club, Pre-School Story Hour, and Children's Art classes at the Toledo Art Museum. Other encouraging signs of increasing community interest was the formation of a Coordinating Council of Agencies and the volunteer service of the American Association of University Women in initiating the Pre-School Story Hour.

Thus, the major innovation in this year's Title I program is the inclusion of the necessary funds for underwriting the cost of inaugurating a full scale Community School program in the Lincoln and Orchard Schools. Students from St. Joseph parochial school will also be asked to participate in the activities.

STAFF

Community School Agent

A full-time community school agent will be hired to work with the principals of the two buildings and community representatives from the area to be served in the development of a comprehensive Community School program. Fully recognizing that the child is the product of his *total* environment, it then becomes the prime responsibility of the Community School Agent to identify community needs and work with whatever agencies necessary in programming for their fulfillment.

Community Agent Assistant for Orchard School

Since the projected program involves two separate schools, the necessity of having a responsible person available at all times that the school is open beyond the regular school day is obvious. This individual (possibly an Orchard faculty member) will be hired by the Community Agent, and his services contracted for the year. It will be his responsibility to be present at Orchard School whenever the school is open for any phase of the Community School Program. He will assume responsibility for seeing that all rooms are left in satisfactory order for school the following day.

Secretary

A part-time secretary (possibly a co-op girl) will be hired for the Community School Agent and will be responsible for providing whatever clerical help necessary. This will include typing, maintenance of records of expenditures, all necessary staff records including hours worked, wages earned, etc.

OPERATIONAL BUDGET

Since at this point and time it is somewhat difficult to anticipate the extent to which people will become involved in projected activities, any amount of money set aside for program operation has to be viewed as strictly an estimate. Since present plans anticipate four separate sessions, each of which would include instructional salaries plus class materials, it is evident that the $1,200 budgeted might prove wholly inadequate. The Board of Education will absorb the maintenance cost created by additional heating and lighting demands.

PROGRAMMING

The community school program year will be composed of four phases:

1. Fall Program –   8 weeks in duration–Student Enrichment and Adult activities
2. Winter Program –   8 weeks in duration–Student Enrichment and Adult activities
3. Spring Program –   10 weeks in duration–Student Enrichment and Adult activities
4. Summer Program – 8 weeks in duration–Student Recreation and Enrichment

Student Enrichment Activities

The major portion of the Student Enrichment activities will be held immediately after school. Some enrichment classes could be held on Saturday, depending upon demand. Since insecurity and hostility toward school often characterize the disadvantaged child, it is important that experiences be provided that will make him feel at ease and look on school as a place he enjoys attending. In light of this, some of the proposed enrichment activities are:

Woodworking for Boys	Fun with Cooking for Boys
Woodworking for Girls	Science Club
Folk Music	Photography Club
Sewing for Fun	Folk Guitar
Reading for Fun	Pre-School Story Hour
Math for Fun	Ceramics
	Individual Tutoring

Recreational Activities

It is imperative that recreational activities be provided to meet the needs of both the adults and children in the immediate neighborhood. Since an extensive recreational program is already provided by the Monroe Recreation Commission and the East End Recreation Center, it will require close coordination and a cooperative effort on the part of the involved agencies. The Community Agent will only offer such activities as are not already provided, avoiding any duplication, and yet making sure the people in the immediate area have the opportunity for a broad and varied recreational program. Some of the projected activities at the present time are:

Teen Club	Boys' Gymnastics
Volleyball	Roller Skating
Men's Club	Social Dancing
Slimnastics for Women	Square Dancing
Movie Program (Sat. A.M.)	

Adult Activities

The initial offerings for adults will be chiefly along the line of recreational and hobby activities, thereby encouraging adult participation. Only as the present alienation against the school is overcome and the adults in the area begin to look on the school in a more favorable attitude will it be possible to offer more along the line of cultural and educational classes which will give the adults in the area a broader area of interests. Some of the possible offerings for next year are:

General Sewing	Class for Expectant Parents
Knitting	Woodworking for Women
Crewel Embroidery	Woodworking for Men
Cake Decorating	Folk Guitar
Furniture Upholstering	Basic Cooking

Summer Program

The summer program will involve students from the immediate area and would offer a variety of arts and crafts, recreational activities, and programming for individual help for students in whatever subject matter found necessary.

A TYPICAL DAY

Day	School	3:30 to 4:30 P.M.	7:00 to 9:00 P.M.
Monday	Lincoln	Reading for Fun (5th-6th)	Roller Skating
		3rd-4th Recreation	General Sewing
		Photography Club	Woodworking for Men
		Individual Tutoring	Folk Guitar
	Orchard	1st-2nd Recreation	Knitting
		Papier Mâché-Pottery (3rd)	Furniture Upholstery

Only as a Community School Program is implemented and adults and children have an opportunity to express their needs and desires is it possible to specifically identify the exact kinds and number of class offerings. At present it is only possible to try to anticipate what offerings will be most in demand basing our projections on the types of interests expressed by neighborhood residents who were involved in our programs this year, such as Mother's Hour and the parent meetings. There is little doubt that by far the biggest job of the Community Agent during the initial year of the program will be to establish rapport with various factions and agencies in the community, identify community needs and get the people of the area involved in his program.

A detailed budget, estimating and defining costs, accompanied the proposal. The total operational budget included a breakdown of areas that would be underwritten by the Board of Education. Government officials rightly feel that local districts should provide resources to help meet the needs of their educationally deprived children. Assuming obligation for some of the financing indicates a genuine concern and effort on the part of the local Board.

ADMINISTERING FEDERALLY FINANCED PROGRAMS

The approval of a project proposal is only the beginning for the principal. He plays an important part in determining how well the project does what it was intended to do. Goverment agencies responsible for program evaluation clearly state the role of administration.

> ...certification requirements place a major responsibility for insuring the proper use of...funds on the local school officials who are, in the final analysis, responsible for seeing that the project is properly prepared and carried out.[4]

The leadership of the principal in encouraging experimentation and instituting reform will determine how soon and how effectively new approaches are embraced and instituted by the staff.

Spending Funds Wisely

The proper use of funds is not always an easy matter for the principal. In the area of equipment and materials, there are requests from all sides, each certain that his wants are justified and should have priority attention. Unless the principal and staff have clear-cut goals for the spending of funds, misunderstanding and friction can develop. What areas will receive first attention, and amounts that will go for expanding, enriching and changing save many headaches when they are clearly delineated.

Staying within the budget poses difficulties also. Without careful consideration it is easy to overstate the needs for one area and shortchange another. This leads to account juggling and proposal amendments or last minute spending in some areas that might suffer in the light of careful educational evaluation. Establishing a spending pattern for the year is helpful in running a smooth operation. Some areas will require large initial purchases, others may require more near the end of the year, while some programs lend themselves to expenditure of near equal amounts monthly. Money is important in making the program go, and

[4]*Ibid*, p. 36.

when the principal knows how, when and where it goes, the program goes better.

<h2 align="right">Other Aspects of Administration</h2>

Since a major responsibility for a program's operation rests with the principal, it is expected that he will be aware of all regulations pertaining to the grant. Knowing limitations and eligibilities can save wasted time and effort. Making requests that are not allowable are certain to raise doubts as to the quality of leadership, if not intentions.

Reports are necessary concomitants of government grants and, while many administrators have the opinion they are excessive, application for a grant implies that all required reports will be given thorough and professional treatment. Thorough record keeping at the local level assures that necessary data will be available when government reports are due. Procrastination and "guesstimating" are not only less than professional, but can make the visit of a government supervisor dreaded, rather than the opportunity to say, "Look what we've been able to accomplish so far."

The best planning cannot foresee all obstacles. The effective principal expects some barriers, indeed, he is constantly seeking means of overcoming weaknesses and increasing the program's effectiveness. He should not approach a major obstacle with the idea that "I'll handle this alone." Seeking the help of others guarantees alternate approaches and the important success criterion of involvement.

As the project moves into high gear new light will be shed. The need for new materials, personnel and in-service programs may crop up. In some cases the need for a major revision in program operation could occur. One mistake doesn't throw a whole project down the drain. Happily, experimentation and innovation rank high in proposed use of Title I funds. The tragic error would be to retain an ineffective program. The principal supervising programs for the deprived should bear in mind the wit's observation: "Few things work the same for everybody. The Eskimos derive the same gratification by rubbing noses."

<h2 align="right">Coordinating Federal Programs</h2>

The principal of a disadvantaged school is in an ideal position to maximize the benefits of all federally funded programs in his school. Through careful planning the various Titles can be used to develop a comprehensive program necessary to attack the many educational problems of the poor or to concentrate most resources on one vital area such as reading.

The following example is one instance of how this might be accomplished.

ESEA Title II funds, designed primarily for library acquisition, could be used to purchase the kinds of books—fast-paced, masculinized, high-interest, low-difficulty—that disadvantaged children want to read. Many of these books could be of a nature to supplement new program approaches such as individualized reading, possible under ESEA Title I funding.

NDEA Title III allotments could concentrate on charts, filmstrips, slides, transparencies, recordings and realia so necessary for concrete experiences for children who lack symbol subtleties and backgrounds in abstractions.

If the local community has a Community Action Program funded through the Office of Economic Opportunity, the fullest communication and cooperation should occur.

Providing work-training experiences through the Neighborhood Youth Corps is one way the school and O.E.O. program can work together. The value of having striving, earning Neighborhood Youth Corps models in the school should not be downgraded. They provide proof for elementary children that their lot is not hopeless and education is not fruitless; that help is available for those willing to help themselves.

Evaluating Programs

Responsible agencies are much concerned with evaluation of program objectives and operation. The following excerpt from NDEA Title III Guidelines is similar to evaluative procedures of other Title programs.

> The State plan must provide for an administrative review at least annually of the programs and operations conducted under the plan. The purpose of the review is to appraise both quantitively and qualitatively the status of the programs and their administration in terms of the State plan's objectives and other provisions. The results and findings of the State Agency's administrative review and evaluation of the total Title III program for the year and of its separate parts, as set forth in the State plan, are to be included in the annual narrative report to the U.S. Commissioner of Education.
>
> In addition to a review of the organization, staffing, fiscal procedures, supervisory program, and other State level activities, the projects approved during the year should be analyzed in relation to State priorities and standards so that projected activities may be planned to meet the greatest need.
>
> The major job in evaluation, however, is the assessment of the effect which the State's Title III program has had on instruction in the classrooms. A

State should be guided by the question, "Has instruction been improved and strengthened?" In seeking to answer this question evaluative techniques such as the following might be used:

- Achievement testing
- Case studies of a limited number of significant projects
- School reports of progress toward short- and long-range instructional goals
- Evaluative studies by research department in local school district
- School visits and interviews with principals, teachers, students, and parents
- Use of check-lists by teachers and principals concerning improvements in course organization, adequacy of equipment and physical facilities, use of modern instructional materials and learning aids, and growth in teacher competency
- Collection of data concerning percentage of students continuing to advanced courses, increased offerings and enrollments, lengthened sequences of study, reduction in number of dropouts, improved teacher qualifications, and improved learning conditions[5]

The government's concern for evaluation should be shared equally by principals and teachers involved in the program's operation. If a program is failing in the function, the principal and his staff should be the first to know and take corrective measures.

It can be readily discerned that most of these suggested evaluative techniques are simple and require no expert knowledge of sophisticated research techniques. Close observation, efficient record keeping and pre- and post-testing are sufficient to meet evaluative requirements. However, if a research specialist is available, his services provide statistical evidence to support observation and other data.

As an example, the abridged evaluation that follows was done by a research coordinator. In all the questions, percentages were enough to indicate some program weaknesses. However, statistical analysis further substantiated the fact that some changes should be initiated.

AFTER-SCHOOL ACTIVITY PERIOD EVALUATION[6]

An after-school *activity period* was offered during the school year in which students were given the opportunity to take classes in things not often thought to be part of regular school. The basic objective of the program was: to improve the children's attitudes toward school and teachers. To evaluate whether the objective was met, attendance was taken and an interest inventory was administered.

[5] *Ibid,* p. 10.

[6] Frederick Robert Wilson, Coordinator of Educational Research, Monroe Public Schools, Monroe, Michigan.

The first three questions asked about the value of the organizational format selected for the activity periods.

QUESTION 1:   Some student have said that we changed classes too often. Others have said that they would have liked to change the things they were taking more often than we did. How did you feel about this?

	Number	*percent*
We changed classes too often	30	12.3%
We changed classes often enough	166	68.5%
We changed classes too few times	46	19.2%

QUESTION 2:   Thinking now about the length of time you had to spend in your class activity, did you feel that the amount of time was too short or too long?

	Number	*Percent*
The amount of time was too short	103	42.7%
The amount of time was just right	122	50.6%
The amount of time was too long	16	6.7%

QUESTION 3:   Try to remember the number of activities offered this year and tell us whether the number of choices offered was too many or too few.

	Number	*Percent*
There were too many things to choose from	22	9.3%
There were just about the right number of activities to choose from	143	60.5%
There were too few things to choose from	71	30.1%

Each child had opportunities to choose his activity for two consecutive opportunity periods. We asked the child to tell us how satisfied he was with his choice for each of these two activity periods.

QUESTION 4:   Thinking back to the first activity you chose, were you glad that you chose it?

	Number	*Percent*
I was very happy with the first activity I chose to be in	139	60.5%
I was happy with it at first but did not like it after a while	55	24.4%
I was mad that I got stuck in it at first but changed my mind later	10	4.4%
I never liked the first activity I was in	25	10.7%
	229	

QUESTION 5:   Now, how about the second opportunity you chose to be in?

	Number	Percent
I was very happy with the second activity I chose to be in	130	81.3%
I was happy with it at first but did not like it after a while	14	8.7%
I was mad that I got stuck in it at first but changed my mind later	11	6.9%
I never liked the second activity I was in	5	3.1%
	160	

The final question asked for suggestions as to the number of times to hold activity periods if the program were to be run again.

QUESTION 6: We would like your suggestions about how often to have the activity periods next year.

	Number	Percent
We should have them once per week	33	13.6%
We should have them twice per week	63	25.9%
We should have them three times per week...........................	147	60.5%
	243	

If it is fair to assume that the answers to questions one, two, and three should be normally distributed with the majority of the children selecting the middle option of each question, the remainder being evenly distributed between the two extreme options, then one may test the answers to the question against the normally distributed expectations to determine an interpretative guide.

QUESTION 1: Frequency of Changing Classes.

	Changed too Often	Changed Often Enough	Changed too Few Times	Total
Observed Freq.	30	166	46	242
Normal Distrib.	38	165	38	
Difference	- 8	1	8	

Chi: 3.380	df: 2	P: .10

There is no difference between the distribution of responses on the questionnaire and the distribution normally expected indicating that by and large people were satisfied with the frequency of class changes.

QUESTION 2: Length of Class Time.

	Time was Too Short	Time was Just Right	Time was Too Long	Total
Observed Freq.	103	122	16	241
Normal Distrib.	38	165	38	
Difference	65	- 43	- 22	

Chi: 135.127	df: 2	p: .001

A strong significant difference is found for this question between the observed and expected frequencies. The major source of the deviation from normality is the 65 cases above the expected frequency saying that the time was too short.

QUESTION 3:   Number of Activities.

	Too Many Choices	Just Right	Too Few Choices	Total
Observed Freq.	22	143	71	236
Normal Distrib.	37	161	37	
Difference	-15	-18	34	

Chi: 58.080   df: 2   p: .001

A strong significant difference is found for this question between the observed and expected frequencies. The major source of the deviation from normality is the 34 cases above the expected frequency saying there were too few choices.

Evaluation without action is a useless enterprise. As a result of this particular report changes were instituted:

- more activities were offered
- participants were given a trial period before settling on a choice

While the participants indicated in question two that time for the activities (one hour) was too short, teachers were unavailable in the number needed for more than this time. This fact was explained to the participants.

Coming on the heels of a school day, an interpretation could be drawn that the desire for lengthier periods indicated pupil enjoyment.

Question six also revealed pupil acceptance and gave advance notice that plans for a more extensive program should be explored.

Those who play the "numbers game" know that federally financed programs have made an impact on meeting the needs of disadvantaged children. Much more can be accomplished if old, unsuccessful methods are scrapped in favor of innovative and coordinated attacks against unique educational problems of the poor.

SUMMARY

The purpose of federal aid to education is chiefly to improve the quality of education. Title I of the Elementary and Secondary Act of 1965 is concerned with meeting the special educational needs of disadvantaged children. Program failures are due to many reasons but lack of innovative approaches stands high on the list.

When writing a proposal, established priorities and standards should be observed. Establishment of need for a program is a key factor in gaining approval. An actual proposal is helpful in illustrating acceptable format and one is included in this chapter for this purpose.

The major responsibility for program operation rests on the principal. Clear-cut goals for expenditure of funds should be established and understood by those involved in the program. Observing regulations and executing forms are understood responsibilities when funds are requested. When possible, all federally funded programs should be coordinated to develop a comprehensive program.

The evaluation of programs should be an ongoing process. Techniques employed can be simple as long as they are thorough. However, if research specialists are available, their services should be utilized to support "on-the-job" findings.

14

Measuring Results and Planning for the Future

When the last dismissal bell rings in June, the principal gains time to reflect on the year just passed and plan for the one ahead. There is value in looking back. Two equally important questions that should be asked are: Where were those areas that proceeded according to plan and were successful? Where were the areas of weakness? The type of planning and action that follows the answers, especially to the latter question, will make a difference in the effectiveness of next year's program.

Some Ways of Looking Back

Some problems have a way of cropping up over and over. A couple of hours spent reading the weekly bulletins will reveal many concerns, both principal and teacher, that were important enough to receive mention more than once during the year. A careful analysis of these recurring "burrs" may suggest a revision of present procedure or an entirely new approach.

Weekly bulletins should also be scanned to critically evaluate the content and style. During the year did it deteriorate into the principal's "harp" sheet? A comparison of September and May bulletins should reveal about the same amount devoted to staff concerns and accomplishments.

Staff meeting minutes reveal, in a nutshell, the history of the important events of the school year and should be considered required reading by every principal.

Staff concerns and recommendations should be abundant in these pages. In looking at things from the "teacher's side," the principal may find ways of easing some friction points. Caught up in the press of the immediate, many good teacher ideas and valid concerns must be shunted aside during the year. June affords a longer look and time to incorporate suggestions and plans for action against more minor teacher troubles.

Perusal of staff meeting minutes will clearly show if they were strictly a principal's forum or truly, as the name implies, sessions in which the total staff were involved.

Committee reports that sometimes received less than proper attention during the hustle and bustle of the year deserve another reading. Views and opinions of committee members, incomplete work and ongoing efforts can help in formulating plans. A thorough knowledge of the various committees' work and written appreciation for individual efforts can assure willing future committee participation.

Behind the cold hard figures of attendance are the very human reasons of regular or irregular patterns.

If there was an increase or decrease in attendance, what were the reasons for it? What methods were successful in increasing attendance? Could they be further emphasized in the coming year? Was every avenue explored in getting the hard core attendance problems to school? Once in the classroom, what approaches were utilized to motivate them to stay?

These, and other searching questions, must be asked and answered if this important factor of school success is to receive its proper attention.

Since discipline occupies so much of the principal's time during the school year, it would be illogical for him to ignore the file of written discipline referrals. After careful study, totally unsuspected patterns may emerge from an individual or a class as a whole. As an example, Johnny had eight referrals, seven of them occurring in physical education. Was Johnny unable to compete with his peers and used inappropriate behavior as a defense? Or was there a personality conflict between him and the teacher? The answer can lead to better school adjustment for Johnny and a saving of the principal's time in the upcoming year.

In the same vein, referrals from a class may reveal most discipline problems occuring over one type of behavior or at a particular time during the day. Many possibilities present themselves. Perhaps a new teaching or organizational approach might alleviate the situation; or a teacher-principal discussion might reveal inordinate stress on some aspect of classroom behavior. Whatever the decision, projected action made in the quietness of June may prove more workable than that sandwiched between a daily menu of September or December problems.

WRAPPING UP THE SCHOOL YEAR

Few areas of school administration can be neatly packaged at the end of the year. The same needs and problems arise year after year and a continuity of thought and action is necessary to meet them. However, there are myriad things that must be done to offically close out the school year.

Priority Attention Concerns

Early attention should be given to unfilled teacher vacancies. Presenting an analysis of the needs of each vacancy to the Director of Personnel may save hiring someone who would be completely out of place. Asking to sit in on candidate interviews is good administrative sense. It is far better to give up a few hours of summer relaxation than to take the chance of days of frustration caused by a teacher misassignment.

The quicker orders for textbooks and supplies are submitted, the better the chances are they will have arrived in August.

Teacher requests should be given careful attention. Quantity and cost should not be the only yardsticks. Appropriateness of materials for the children in question should receive major consideration.

Physical surroundings are factors in learning, and to some degree, the teachers' and pupils' state of mind. A leaky radiator, a stuck window and other ubiquitous building flaws become irritants during the year that may sometimes affect teacher performance. Asking teachers for a list of needed room repairs and developing a custodians' list of needed work allows for proper summer maintenance.

Teacher opinions should be solicited and followed where feasible. For example, if rooms are to be painted, it is a diplomatic move to allow teachers affected to name their choice of room color.

Putting on the Finishing Touches

June duties that appear mundane should not be taken lightly. For instance, rubber stamping the exact menus that brought protests from parents and pupils a year earlier may lead to uncomfortable situations in the year ahead. Few pupils are enthusiastic about cafeteria food, but if a close look at meals reveals the food to be lacking in variety and attractiveness heed should be paid to their complaints.

Despite all the enticements June days offer, the principal should carefully cover every aspect of school operation before calling it quits for the summer.

Looking at transportation may bring about a decision to make different bus route assignments.

Danger spots, unsupervised by crossing guards, may lead to some planned action; examination of handbooks will probably suggest revisions; gauging staff strengths may result in a shuffling of room assignments; the playground, parent organizations, pupil room placement; after-school activities and summer activities, all these must come in for their fair share of the principal's consideration.

The wrap-up of the year's activities is little different from a football coach viewing game movies. In the playback he sees both strengths and weaknesses and formulates a game plan designed to eliminate previous errors and capitalize on strengths.

The Principal's Plans

Every principal should know how to play. If he becomes so tied up in his job that he can't enjoy life outside his office, he actually loses some effectiveness. By virtue of his position the principal's day is largely taken with problems. He is in danger of losing perspective unless he associates with others in recreational activities.

Summer's change-of-pace has a way of refueling enthusiasm for the year ahead. As July slips into August, the "typical" principal finds new ideas and plans for initiating them coming to mind. As August moves toward September, there is a growing eagerness to get back into the job and on with his business of educating children.

When the first bell of the year rings he is ready for action, certain that this new year will be the most fruitful he has ever experienced.

SUMMARY

At the end of the school year the principal should ask: In what areas were we successful and where did we fail? Plans to minimize weaknesses and maximize strengths should be made.

Looking through the year's weekly bulletins and staff meeting minutes will reveal many areas of concern and suggest means of correcting them. Attendance figures and discipline referrals are other means of analyzing key areas of school operation.

In closing the school year, unfilled teacher vacancies, ordering textbooks and supplies, and setting up a summer maintenance schedule should receive early attention.

As onerous as year-end work may be, old plans should not be retained merely for the sake of saving time and work.

The principal's summer plans should include time for rest and relaxation. Time away from the job has the salubrious effect of creating new zest and enthusiasm for the year ahead.

Index